A CONCISE

LINCOLN DICTIONARY

Thoughts and Statements

A CONCISE

LINCOLN DICTIONARY

Thoughts and Statements

Compiled and Arranged

by

RALPH B. WINN

PHILOSOPHICAL LIBRARY

New York

ACKNOWLEDGMENTS

I am grateful to all the publishers and editors who have kindly granted us permission to quote John Dewey's words from their books, namely to: Appleton-Century-Crofts from *The Educational Frontier;* the Beacon Press from *Knowing and the Known* and *Reconstruction in Philosophy;* Columbia University Press from *Construction and Criticism* and "Antinaturalism in Extremis" found in *Naturalism and the Human Spirit;* E. P. Dutton and Company from *Schools of Tomorrow;* Harcourt, Brace and Company from "A Critique of American Civilization" included in *Recent Gains of American Civilization* (edited by K. Page); Harper and Brothers from *Psychology;* Harvard University Press from "Authority and Social Change" included in the tercentenary volume on *Authority and the Individual;* C. C. Heath and Company from *How We Think;* Henry Holt and Company from *Characters and Events, Ethics* (with J. H. Tufts), *Human Nature and Conduct, The Influence of Darwin on Philosophy, Logic: the Theory of Inquiry, The Public and its Problems,* and also from *The Philosophy of John Dewey* (edited by J. Ratner) and "The

− A −

ABOLITION

1. Be it enacted by the Senate and House of Representatives of the United States, in Congress assembled, That no person not now within the District of Columbia, nor now owned by any person or persons now residing within it, nor hereafter born within it, shall ever be held in slavery within said District.— *Bill to Abolish Slavery* (Sec. 1), January 16, 1849.

2. I, Abraham Lincoln, President of the United States of America, and commander-in-chief of the army and navy thereof, do hereby proclaim and declare . . . That on the first day of January, in the year of our Lord one thousand eight hundred and sixty-three, all persons held as slaves within any State or designated part of a State the people whereof shall then be in rebellion against the United States, shall be then, thenceforward, and forever free; and the Executive Department of the United States, including the military and naval authority thereof, will recognize and maintain the freedom of such persons,

and will do no act or acts to repress such persons, or any of them, in any efforts they may make for their actual freedom.—*Preliminary Emancipation Proclamation*, September 22, 1862.

3. Among the friends of the Union there is great diversity of sentiment and of policy in regard to slavery and the African race amongst us. Some would perpetuate slavery; some would abolish it suddenly and without compensation; some would remove the freed people from us, and some would retain them with us; and there are yet other minor diversities. Because of these diversities we waste much strength in struggles among ourselves. By mutual concession we should harmonize and act together. This would be compromise; but it would be compromise among the friends, and not with the enemies of the Union—*Annual Message to Congress*, December 1, 1862.

4. By virtue of the power and for the purpose aforesaid, I do order and declare that all persons held as slaves within said designated States and parts of States are, and henceforward shall be, free; and that the executive Government of the United States, including the military and naval authorities thereof, will recognize and maintain the freedom of said persons.

And I hereby enjoin upon people so declared to be free to abstain from all violence, unless in necessary self-defense; and I recommend to them that, in all cases where allowed, they labor faithfully for reasonable wages.

And I further declare and make known that such persons of suitable condition will be received into the armed service of the United States to garrison forts, positions, stations, and other places, and to man vessels of all sorts in said service.

And upon this act, sincerely believed to be an act of justice, warranted by the Constitution upon military necessity, I invoke the considerate judgment of mankind and the gracious favor of Almighty God.—*Emancipation Proclamation*, January 1, 1863.

SEE ALSO: Emancipation; Negroes; Party 2; Slavery.

ACTION

1. Tell him, when he starts, to put it through—not to be writing or telegraphing back here, but put it through.—*Letter to Secretary S. Cameron*, June 20, 1861.

2. He who does *something* at the head of one Regiment, will eclipse him who does *nothing* at the head of a hundred.—*A Letter to D. Hunter*, December 31, 1861.

3. I shall do more whenever I shall believe doing more will help the cause.—*Letter to C. D. Robinson*, August 17, 1864.

SEE ALSO: Fashion; Majority 4; Selfishness 1.

AGITATORS

Must I shoot a simple-minded soldier boy who deserts, while I must not touch a hair of a wily agitator who induces him to desert? This is none the less injurious when effected by getting a father, or brother, or friend into a public meeting, and there working upon his feelings till he is persuaded to write the soldier boy that he is fighting in a bad cause, for a wicked administration of a contemptible government, too weak to arrest and punish him if he shall desert. I think that, in such a case, to silence the agitator and save the boy is not only constitutional, but withal a great mercy.—*Letter to E. Corning and Others,* June 12, 1863.

SEE ALSO: Cause and Effect.

AMBITION

1. Every man is said to have his peculiar ambition. Whether it be true or not, I can say, for one, that I have no other so great as that of being truly esteemed of my fellow-men, by rendering myself worthy of their esteem. How far I shall succeed in gratifying this ambition is yet to be developed.— *Address to the People of Sangamon County,* March 9, 1832.

2. It is to deny what the history of the world tells us is true, to suppose that men of ambition and talents will not continue to spring up amongst us. And when they do, they will as naturally seek the gratification of their ruling passion as others have done before them.—*Lyceum Address,* January 27, 1837.

SEE ALSO: Government 1; Mob Law 1.

4

AMENDMENTS

1. I wish now to submit a few remarks on the general proposition of amending the Constitution. As a general rule, I think we would much better let it alone. No slight occasion should tempt us to touch it. Better not take the first step, which may lead to a habit of altering it. Better, rather, habituate ourselves to think of it as unalterable. It can scarcely be made better than it is. New provisions would introduce new difficulties, and thus create an increased appetite for further change.—*Speech in the U.S. House of Representatives,* June 20, 1848.

2. I cannot be ignorant of the fact that many worthy and patriotic citizens are desirous of having the National Constitution amended. While I make no recommendation of amendments, I fully recognize the rightful authority of the people over the whole subject, to be exercised in either of the modes prescribed in the instrument itself; and I should, under existing circumstances, favor rather than oppose a fair opportunity being afforded the people to act upon it.—*First Inaugural Address,* March 4, 1861.

SEE ALSO: Constitution 1; People 4.

AMERICA

In the great journal of things happening under the sun, we, the American people, find our account running under date of the nineteenth century of the Christian era. We find ourselves in the peaceful possession of the fairest portion of the earth as regards

5

extent of territory, fertility of soil, and salubrity of climate. We find ourselves under the government of a system of political institutions conducing more essentially to the ends of civil and religious liberty than any of which the history of former times tells us. We, when mounting the stage of existence, found ourselves the legal inheritors of these fundamental blessings. We toiled not in the acquirement or establishment of them; they are a legacy bequeathed us by a once hardy, brave, and patriotic, but now lamented and departed, race of ancestors. Theirs was the task (and nobly they performed it) to possess themselves, and through themselves us, of this goodly land, and to uprear upon its hills and its valleys a political edifice of liberty and equal rights; 'tis ours only to transmit these—the former unprofaned by the foot of an invader, the latter undecayed by the lapse of time and untorn by usurpation—to the latest generation that fate shall permit the world to know. This task of gratitude to our fathers, justice to ourselves, duty to posterity, and love for our species in general, all imperatively require us faithfully to perform.

How then shall we perform it? At what point shall we expect the approach of danger? By what means shall we fortify against it? Shall we expect some transatlantic military giant to step the ocean and crush us at a blow? Never! All the armies of Europe, Asia, and Africa combined, with all the treasure of the earth (our own excepted) in their military chest, with a Bonaparte for a commander, could not by force take a drink from the Ohio or make a track on the Blue Ridge in a trial of a thousand years.

At what point, then, is the approach of danger to be expected? I answer, If it ever reach us it must spring up amongst us; it cannot come from abroad. If destruction be our lot we must ourselves be its author and finisher. As a nation of freemen we must live through all time, or die by suicide.

I hope I am over wary; but if I am not, there is even now something of ill omen amongst us. I mean the increasing disregard for law which pervades the country—the growing disposition to substitute the wild and furious passions in lieu of the sober judgment of courts.—*Lyceum Address,* January 27, 1837.

SEE ALSO: Union; Women.

AMNESTY

1. I, Abraham Lincoln, President of the United States, do proclaim, declare, and make known to all persons who have, directly or by implication, participated in the existing rebellion, except as hereinafter excepted, that a full pardon is hereby granted to them and each of them, with restoration of all rights of property, except as to slaves, and in property cases where rights of third parties shall be intervened, and upon the condition that every such person shall take and subscribe an oath, and thenceforward keep and maintain said oath inviolate; and which oath shall be registered for permanent preservation. . . .

The persons exempted from the benefits of the

7

foregoing provisions are all who are, or shall have been, civil or diplomatic officers or agents of the so-called Confederate Government; all who have left judicial stations under the United States to aid the rebellion; all who are or shall have been military or naval officers of said so-called Confederate Government above the rank of colonel in the army or of lieutenant in the navy; all who left seats in the United States Congress to aid the rebellion; all who resigned commissions in the army or navy of the United States and afterward aided the rebellion; and all who have engaged in any way in treating colored persons, or white persons in charge of such, otherwise than lawfully as prisoners of war.—*Proclamation of Amnesty and Reconstruction,* December 8, 1863.

2. When a man is sincerely penitent for his misdeeds, and gives satisfactory evidence of the same, he can safely be pardoned, and there is no exception to the rule.—*Remark to White House Group,* April 30, 1864.

ARMY

1. With us every soldier is a man of character, and must be treated with more consideration than is customary in Europe.—*Letter to Count Gasparin,* August 4, 1862.

2. Armies, the world over, destroy enemies' property when they cannot use it; and even destroy their own to keep it from the enemy. Civilized belligerents do all in their power to help themselves or hurt the

enemy, except a few things regarded as barbarous or cruel. Among the exceptions are the massacre of vanquished foes and non-combatants, male or female.— *Letter to J. C. Conkling,* August 26, 1863.

SEE ALSO: Authority; Liberty 4; Soldiers; Thanksgiving.

ATHEISM

I can see how it might be possible for a man to look down upon the earth and be an atheist, but I cannot conceive how he could look up into the heavens and say there is no God.—*Quoted in the Reader's Digest,* February, 1947.

AUTHORITY

It has been said that one bad general is better than two good ones; and the saying is true, if taken to mean no more than that an army is better directed by a single mind, though inferior, than by two superior ones, at variance and cross-purposes with each other. And the same is true in all joint operations wherein those engaged can have none but a common end in view, and can differ only as to the choice of means. In a storm at sea, no one on board can wish the ship to sink; and yet, not unfrequently, all go down together, because too many will direct, and no single mind can be allowed to control.—*Annual Message to Congress,* December 3, 1861.

SEE ALSO: Immigrants 2; National Bank 2; Peace 4; Reason 3.

BALLOTS

1. Do not mistake that the ballot is stronger than the bullet. Therefore, let the legions of slavery use bullets; but let us wait patiently till November and fire ballots at them in return; and by that peaceful policy, I believe we shall ultimately win.—*The "Lost" Speech at Bloomington,* May 29, 1856.

2. To give the victory to the right, not bloody bullets, but peaceful ballots only are necessary. Thanks to our good old Constitution, and organization under it, these alone are necessary.—*Notes for Speeches,* c. October 1, 1858.

3. Our popular government has often been called an experiment. Two points in it our people have already settled—the successful establishing and the successful administering of it. One still remains—its successful maintenance against a formidable internal attempt to overthrow it. It is now for them to demonstrate to the world that those who can fairly carry an election can also suppress a rebellion; that ballots

are the rightful and peaceful successors of bullets; and that when ballots have fairly and constitutionally decided, there can be no successful appeal, except to ballots themselves, at succeeding elections. Such will be a great lesson of peace: teaching men that what they cannot take by an election, neither can they take it by a war.—*Message to Congress,* July 4, 1861.

SEE ALSO: Voting.

BIBLE

It is the best gift God has given to men. All the good Savior gave to the world was communicated through this book. But for it we could not know right from wrong. All things most desirable for man's welfare, here and hereafter, are to be found portrayed in it.—*Reply to Committee presenting Bible,* September 9, 1864.

SEE ALSO: History 1; Property 2.

BOOKS

1. It is of no consequence to be in a large town while you are reading. . . . The books, and your capacity for understanding them, are just the same in all places.—*Letter to I. Reavis,* November 5, 1855.

2. Books serve to show a man that those original thoughts of his aren't very new, after all.—*A Remark,* 1861, *according to C. Sandburg's War Years, II, p.* 309.

SEE ALSO: Reading.

11

BORROWING

As an individual who undertakes to live by borrowing soon finds his original means devoured by interest, and next, no one left to borrow from, so must it be with a government.—*Whig Circular,* March 4, 1843.

BUSINESS

1. If I be asked whether I would destroy all commerce, I answer, Certainly not; I would continue it where it is necessary, and discontinue it where it is not. An instance: I would continue commerce so far as it is employed in bringing us coffee, and I would discontinue it so far as it is employed in bringing us cotton goods.—*Tariff Memorandum,* December 1, 1847.

2. Few things are so troublesome to the government as the fierceness with which profits in trading are sought.—*Letter to W. Kellogg,* June 29, 1863.

SEE ALSO: Civil War 6; Liquor; War 4.

– C –

CAPITAL

There is one point, with its connections, not so hackneyed as most others, to which I ask a brief attention. It is the effort to place capital on an equal footing with, if not above, labor, in the structure of government. It is assumed that labor is available only in connection with capital; that nobody labors unless somebody else, owning capital, somehow by the use of it, induces him to labor. This assumed, it is next considered whether it is best that capital shall *hire* laborers, and thus induce them to work by their own consent, or *buy* them, and drive them to it without their consent. Having proceeded so far, it is naturally concluded that all laborers are either hired laborers or what we call slaves. And further it is assumed that whoever is once a hired laborer, is fixed in that condition for life. Now, there is no such relation between capital and labor as assumed; nor is there any such thing as a free man being fixed for

13

life in the condition of a hired laborer. Both these assumptions are false, and all inferences from them are groundless. Labor is prior to, and independent of, capital. Capital is only the fruit of labor, and could never have existed if labor had not first existed. Labor is the superior of capital, and deserves much the higher consideration. Capital has its rights, which are as worthy of protection as any other rights. Nor is it denied that there is, and probably always will be, a relation between labor and capital, producing mutual benefits. The error is in assuming that the whole labor of the community exists within that relation.— *Annual Message to Congress,* December 3, 1861.

SEE ALSO: Labor 4, 5; Wealth 1.

CATCH-WORDS

The significance of catch-words cannot pass unheeded, for they constitute a sign of the times. Everything in this world "jibes" in with everything else.— *The "Lost" Speech at Bloomington,* May 29, 1856.

CAUSE AND EFFECT

Like causes produce like effects. . . . Will not the same cause that produced agitation in 1820, when the Missouri Compromise was formed—that which produced the agitation upon the annexation of Texas, and at other times—work out the same results always? Do you think that the nature of man will be changed—that the same causes that produced agitation at one time will not have the same effect at another?—*Reply at Jonesboro Debate,* September 15, 1858.

SEE ALSO: Freedom 3; History 2.

CHANGE

It is said an Eastern monarch once charged his wise men to invent him an aphorism to be ever in view, and which should be true and appropriate in all times and situations. They presented him the words, "And this, too, shall pass away."—*Address before the Wisconsin State Agricultural Society,* September 30, 1859.

SEE ALSO: Human Nature 1.

CHARITY

With malice toward none; with charity for all; with firmness in the right, as God gives us to see the right, let us strive on to finish the work we are in; to bind up the nation's wounds; to care for him who shall have borne the battle, and for his widow, and his orphan—to do all which may achieve and cherish a just and lasting peace among ourselves and with all nations.—*Second Inaugural Address,* March 4, 1865.

SEE ALSO: Negroes 4.

CHILDREN

It is my pleasure that my children are free and happy, and unrestrained by parental tyranny. Love is the chain whereby to bind a child to its parents.—

A Remark, c. 1860, *as reported by W. H. Herndon.*
SEE ALSO: Law 3; Liberty 3.

CHURCH

1. The United States Government must not . . . undertake to run the churches. When an individual in a church or out of it becomes dangerous to the public interest, he must be checked; but let the churches, as such, take care of themselves. It will not do for the United States to appoint trustees, supervisors or other agents for the churches—*Letter to S. R. Curtis,* January 2, 1863.

2. I have never interfered, nor thought of interfering, as to who shall or shall not preach in any church; nor have I knowingly or believingly tolerated anyone else to so interfere by my authority.—*Letter to O. D. Filley,* December 22, 1863.
SEE ALSO: Religion 2, 3.

CITIZENS

Let us neither express nor cherish any hard feelings toward any citizen who by his vote has differed with us. Let us at all times remember that all American citizens are brothers of a common country, and should dwell together in the bonds of fraternal feeling.—*Remark at the Meeting at Springfield,* November 20, 1860.
SEE ALSO: Voting 1; Loyalty 2; Mob Law 1; Justice 4.

CIVILIZATION

From the first appearance of man upon the earth down to very recent times, the words "stranger" and "enemy" were quite or almost synonymous. Long after civilized nations had defined robbery and murder as high crimes, and had affixed severe punishments to them, when practised among and upon their own people respectively, it was deemed no offense, but even meritorious, to rob and murder and enslave strangers, whether as nations or as individuals. Even yet, this has not totally disappeared. The man of the highest moral cultivation, in spite of all which abstract principle can do, likes him whom he does know much better than him whom he does not know. To correct the evils, great and small, which spring from want of sympathy and from positive enmity among strangers, as nations or as individuals, is one of the highest functions of civilization.—*Address before the Wisconsin State Agricultural Society,* September 30, 1859.

SEE ALSO: War 2.

CIVIL WAR

1. On the side of the Union it is a struggle to maintain in the world that form and substance of government whose leading object is to elevate the condition of men, lift artificial burdens from all shoulders and clear the paths of laudable pursuits for all; to afford all an unfettered start and a fair chance

in the race of life. This is the leading object of the government for whose existence we contend.—*Message to Congress,* July 4, 1861.

2. What would you do in my position? Would you drop the war where it is? Or would you prosecute it in future with elderstalk squirts charged with rosewater? Would you deal lighter blows rather than heavier ones? Would you give up the contest, leaving any available means unapplied? I am in no boastful mood. I shall not do more than I can, and I shall do all I can, to save the government, which is my sworn duty as well as my personal inclination. I shall do nothing in malice. What I deal with is too vast for malicious dealing.—*Letter to C. Bullitt,* July 28, 1862.

3. Without the institution of slavery and the colored race as a basis, the war could not have an existence.—*Speech to Free Colored Men,* August 14, 1862.

4. Needful diversions of wealth and of strength from the fields of peaceful industry to the national defense have not arrested the plow, the shuttle or the ship; the ax has enlarged the borders of our settlements, and the mines, as well of iron and coal as of the precious metals, have yielded even more abundantly than heretofore. Population has steadily increased notwithstanding the waste that has been made in the camp, the siege and battlefield, and the country, rejoicing in the consciousness of augmented strength and vigor, is permitted to expect continuance

of years with large increase of freedom.—*Thanksgiving Proclamation*, October 3, 1863.

5. When the war began three years ago, neither party, nor any man, expected it would last till now. Each looked for the end, in some way, long ere to-day. Neither did any anticipate that domestic slavery would be much affected by the war. But here we are; the war has not ended, and slavery has been much affected—how much, needs not now be recounted.—*Address at Sanitary Fair*, April 18, 1864.

6. War, at the best, is terrible, and this war of ours, in its magnitude and its duration, is one of the most terrible. It has deranged business, totally in many localities, and partially in all localities. It has destroyed property and ruined homes; it has produced a national debt and taxation unprecedented, at least in this country; it has carried mourning to almost every home, until it can almost be said that the "Heavens are hung in black."—*Speech at Sanitary Fair*, June 16, 1864.

SEE ALSO: Immigrants 3; Thanksgiving.

CONDUCT

1. I believe it is universally understood and acknowledged that all men will ever act correctly unless they have a motive to do otherwise.—*Bank Speech*, January, 1837.

2. I made a point of honor and conscience in all things to stick to my word, especially if others had

been induced to act upon it.—*Letter to Mrs. O. H. Browning,* April 1, 1838.

3. I wish to do justice to all.—*Speech in Congress,* July 27, 1848.

4. I planted myself upon the truth and the truth only, so far as I know it, or could be brought to know it.—*Springfield Speech,* July 17, 1858.

5. I have never tried to conceal my opinions, nor tried to deceive anyone in reference to them.—*Speech at Freeport,* August 27, 1858.

6. It really hurts me very much to suppose that I have wronged anybody on earth.—*Debate at Quincy,* October 13, 1858.

7. I wish to avoid violations of law and bad faith. —*Letter to General H. W. Halleck,* October 3, 1862.

SEE ALSO: Persuasion.

CONSCIENCE

1. Consciences differ in different individuals.— *Notes for Speeches,* c. October 1, 1858.

2. I desire so to conduct the affairs of this administration that if at the end, when I come to lay down the reins of power, I have lost every other friend on earth, I shall at least have one friend left, and that friend shall be down inside me.—*Reply to Missouri Committee,* 1864.

SEE ALSO: Conduct 2; Politics 2.

CONSERVATISM

1. What is conservatism? Preserving the old against the new.—*Speech at Leavenworth,* December 3, 1859.

2. What is conservatism? Is it not adherence to the old and tried, against the new and untried?—*Address at Cooper Institute,* February 27, 1860.

CONSTITUTION

1. I wish now to submit a few remarks on the general proposition of amending the Constitution. As a general rule, I think we would much better let it alone. No slight occasion should tempt us to touch it. Better not take the first step, which may lead to a habit of altering it. Better, rather, habituate ourselves to think of it as unalterable. It can scarcely be made better than it is. New provisions would introduce new difficulties, and thus create an increased appetite for further change.—*Speech on Internal Improvements,* June 20, 1848.

2. Don't interfere with anything in the Constitution. That must be maintained, for it is the only safeguard of our liberties.—*Speech at Kalamazoo,* August 27, 1856.

3. The Constitution is different in its application in cases of rebellion or invasion, involving the public safety, from what it is in times of profound peace and public security; and this opinion I adhere to simply because, by the Constitution itself, things may be done in the one case which may not be done in the other.—*Letter to M. Birchard and Others,* June 29, 1863.

SEE ALSO: Amendments; Ballots 2; History 1; Liberty 2; National Bank 2; People 3, 4; Reason 1; Right and Wrong 4; Slavery 16; States 3; Union 2, 3, 4.

CORRUPTION

I know that the volcano at Washington, aroused and directed by the evil spirit that reigns there, is belching forth the lava of political corruption in a current broad and deep, which is sweeping with frightful velocity over the whole length and breadth of the land, bidding fair to leave unscathed no green spot of living thing; while on its bosom are riding, like demons on the waves of hell, the imps of that evil spirit, and fiendishly taunting all those who dare resist its destroying course with the hopelessness of their effort.—*Speech on Subtreasury*, December 20, 1839.

SEE ALSO Politics 3.

COWARDICE

If the Lord gives a man a pair of cowardly legs, how can he help their running away with him. . . . A man can't help being a coward any more than he could help being a humpback, if he were born with one.—*Remarks*, September 11, 1863.

SEE ALSO: Party 2.

– D –

DEATH

1. We all feel to know that we have to die. How? We have never died yet. We know it because we know, or at least think we know, that of all the beings, just like ourselves, who have been coming into the world for six thousand years, not one is now living who was here two hundred years ago. I repeat, then, that we know nothing of what will happen in future, but by the analogy of experience.—*Speech on Subtreasury*, December 20, 1839.

2. Death, abstractly considered, is the same with the high as with the low; but practically, we are not so much aroused to the contemplation of our own mortal natures, by the fall of many undistinguished as that of one great and well known name.—*Eulogy on Zachary Taylor*, July 25, 1850.

3. If they kill me, I shall never die another death. —*A Remark to Hannah Armstrong*, February, 1861.

SEE ALSO: Democracy 4.

DECEIT

1. I never encourage deceit, and falsehood, especially if you have got a bad memory, is the worst enemy a fellow can have. The fact is truth is your truest friend, no matter what the circumstances are.— *Letter to G. E. Pickett,* February 22, 1842.

2. You can fool all of the people some of the time, and some of the people all of the time, but you cannot fool all of the people all of the time.—*Speech at Clinton,* September 8, 1858.

SEE ALSO: Conduct 5; War 3.

DECLARATION OF INDEPENDENCE

1. When we were the political slaves of King George, and wanted to be free, we called the maxim that "all men are created equal" a self-evident truth, but now when we have grown fat, and have lost all dread of being slaves ourselves, we have become so greedy to be masters that we call the same maxim "a self-evident lie."—*Letter to G. Robertson,* August 15, 1855.

2. Now, my countrymen, if you have been taught doctrines conflicting with the great landmarks of the Declaration of Independence; if you have listened to suggestions which would take away from its grandeur and mutilate the fair symmetry of its proportions; if you have been inclined to believe that all men are not created equal in those inalienable rights enumerated in our chart of liberty, let me entreat you to come back. Return to the fountain whose

waters spring close by the blood of the revolution. Think nothing of me—take no thought for the political fate of any man whomsoever—but come back to the truths that are in the Declaration of Independence. You may do anything with me you choose, if you will but heed these sacred principles.—*Speech at Lewiston,* August 17, 1858.

3. I have never had a feeling, politically, that did not spring from the sentiments embodied in the Declaration of Independence. I have often pondered over the dangers which were incurred by the men who assembled here and framed and adopted that Declaration. I have pondered over the toils that were endured by the officers and soldiers of the army who achieved that independence. I have often inquired of myself what great principle or idea it was that kept this confederacy so long together. It was not the mere matter of separation of the colonies from the motherland, but that sentiment in the Declaration of Independence which gave liberty not alone to the people of this country, but hope to all the world for all future time. It was that which gave promise that in due time the weights would be lifted from the shoulders of all men, and that all should have an equal chance. This is the sentiment embodied in the Declaration of Independence.—*Independence Hall Address,* February 22, 1861.

SEE ALSO: Equality 4, 7; Liberty 3; Self-government 3.

DEMOCRACY

1. True democracy makes no inquiry about the color of the skin, or place of nativity, or any other similar circumstance or condition.—*Speech at Cincinnati,* May 6, 1842.

2. As I would not be a slave, so I would not be a master. This expresses my idea of democracy. Whatever differs from this, to the extent of the difference, is not democracy.—*A Letter,* c. 1858.

3. The so-called Democracy of today holds . . . the liberty of one man to be absolutely nothing when in conflict with another man's right of property.—*Letter to H. L. Pierce and Others,* April 6, 1859.

4. We cannot dedicate—we cannot consecrate—we cannot hallow—this ground. The brave men, living and dead, who struggled here, have consecrated it far above our poor power to add or detract. The world will little note nor long remember what we say here, but it can never forget what they did here. It is for us, the living, rather, to be dedicated here to the unfinished work which they who fought here have thus far so nobly advanced. It is rather for us to be here dedicated to the great task remaining before us —that from these honored dead we take increased devotion; that we here highly resolve that these dead shall not have died in vain; that this nation, under God, shall have a new birth of freedom; and that the government of the people, by the people, for the people, shall not perish from the earth.—*Gettysburg Address,* November 19, 1863.

SEE ALSO: America.

DESPOTISM

1. When the white man governs himself, that is self-government; but when he governs himself and also governs another man, that is more than self-government—that is despotism.—*Speech at Peoria,* October 16, 1854.

2. In a despotism, one might not wonder to see slavery advance steadily and remorselessly into new dominions; but is it not wonderful, is it not even alarming, to see its steady advance in a land dedicated to the proposition that "all men are created equal?"—*The "Lost" Speech at Bloomington,* May 29, 1856.

3. Destroy this spirit [of liberty] and you have planted the seeds of despotism at your doors. Accustomed to trample on the rights of others, you have lost the genius of your own independence and become fit subjects of the first cunning tyrant who rises among you.—*Speech at Edwardsville,* September 13, 1858.

SEE ALSO: Equality 3; Liberty 4; Majority 2.

DILIGENCE

1. The leading rule for the lawyer, as for the man of every other calling, is diligence. Leave nothing for tomorrow which can be done today. Never let your correspondence fall behind. Whatever piece of business you have in hand, before stopping, do all the labor pertaining to it which can then be done.—*Notes for Law Lecture,* c. July 1, 1850.

2. Let not him who is houseless pull down the house of another, but let him work diligently and

27

build one for himself, thus by example assuring that his own shall be safe from violence when built.— *Reply to New York Workingmen*, March 21, 1864.

SEE ALSO: Property 3.

DUTY

1. If there is anything which it is the duty of the whole people to never entrust to any hands but their own, that thing is the preservation and perpetuity of their own liberties and institutions.—*Speech at Peoria*, October 16, 1854.

2. Let us have faith that right makes might, and in that faith let us to the end dare to do our duty as we understand it.—*Address at Cooper Institute*, February 27, 1860.

3. Eternal right makes might; as we understand our duty, let us do it!—*Hartford Speech*, March 5, 1860.

SEE ALSO: Good and Evil 2; Immigrants 2; Money 2; Progress 3; Right and Wrong 7.

— E —

EDUCATION

1. Upon the subject of education, not presuming to dictate any plan or system respecting it, I can only say that I view it as the most important subject which we as a people can be engaged in. That every man may receive at least a moderate education, and thereby be enabled to read the histories of his own and other countries, by which he may duly appreciate the value of our free institutions, appears to be an object of vital importance, even on this account alone, to say nothing of the advantages and satisfaction to be derived from all being able to read the Scriptures, and other works both of a religious and moral nature, for themselves.

For my part, I desire to see the time when education—and by its means, morality, sobriety, enterprise, and industry—shall become much more general than at present, and should be gratified to have it in my power to contribute something to the advancement of any measure which might have a tendency to accelerate that happy period.—*Address to the People of Sangamon County,* March 9, 1832.

2. Free labor argues that as the Author of man makes every individual with one head and one pair of hands, it was probably intended that heads and hands should cooperate as friends, and that that particular head should direct and control that pair of hands. As each man has one mouth to be fed, and one pair of hands to furnish the food, it was probably intended that that particular pair of hands should feed that particular mouth—that each head is the natural guardian, director and protector of the hands and mouth inseparably connected with it, and that being so, every head should be cultivated and improved by whatever will add to its capacity for performing its charge. In one word, free labor insists on universal education.—*Address before the Wisconsin State Agricultural Society,* September 30, 1859.

SEE ALSO: Law 3; Punctuation; Teaching.

EMANCIPATION

1. So far as peaceful voluntary emancipation is concerned, the condition of the negro slave in America, scarcely less terrible to the contemplation of a free mind, is now as fixed and hopeless of change for the better, as that of the lost souls of the finally impenitent.—*Letter to G. Robertson,* August 15, 1855.

2. There is an objection urged against free colored persons remaining in the country which is largely imaginary, if not sometimes malicious. It is insisted

that their presence would injure and displace white labor and white laborers. . . . Is it true, then, that colored people can displace any more white labor by being free than by remaining slaves? If they stay in their old places, they jostle no white laborers; if they leave their old places, they leave them open to white laborers. Logically, there is neither more nor less of it. Emancipation, even without deportation, would probably enhance the wages of white labor, and very surely would not reduce them. Thus, the customary amount of labor would still have to be performed; the freed people would surely not do more than their old proportion of it, and very probably for a time would do less, leaving an increased part to white laborers, bringing their labor into greater demand, and consequently enhancing the wages of it. With deportation, even to a limited extent, enhanced wages to white labor is mathematically certain. . . .

But it is dreaded that the freed people will swarm forth and cover the whole land. Are they not already in the land? Will liberation make them any more numerous? Equally distributed among the whites of the whole country, there would be but one colored to seven whites. Could the one in any way greatly disturb the seven? There are many communities now having more than one free colored person to seven whites, and this without any apparent consciousness of evil from it.

But why should emancipation south send the free people north? People of any color seldom run un-

31

less there be something to run from. Heretofore colored people, to some extent, have fled north from bondage; and now, perhaps, from both bondage and destitution. But if gradual emancipation and deportation be adopted, they will have neither to flee from. Their old masters will give them wages at least until new laborers can be procured; and the freedmen, in turn, will gladly give their labor for the wages till new homes can be found for them in congenial climes and with people of their own blood and race. The proposition can be trusted on the mutual interests involved. And, in any event, cannot the North decide for itself whether to receive them?—*Annual Message to Congress,* December 1, 1862.

3. The [Emancipation] Proclamation, as law, either is valid or is not valid. If it is not valid it needs no retraction; if it is valid it cannot be retracted any more than the dead can be brought to life.—*Letter to J. C. Conkling,* August 26, 1863.

4. If the people should, by whatever mode or means, make it an executive duty to reenslave such persons, another, and not I, must be their instrument to perform it.—*Annual Message to Congress,* December 6, 1864.

SEE ALSO: Abolition; Negroes; Slavery.

EQUALITY

1. Most governments have been based, practically, on the denial of the equal rights of men, as I have, in part, stated them; ours began by affirming those

rights. They said, some men are too ignorant and vicious to share in government. Possibly so, said we; and, by your system, you would always keep them ignorant and vicious. We proposed to give all a chance; and we expected the weak to grow stronger, the ignorant wiser, and all better and happier together. We made the experiment, and the fruit is before us. Look at it, think of it. Look at it in its aggregate grandeur, of extent of country, and numbers of population—of ship, and steamboat, and railroad.—*A Fragment on Slavery*, c. July 1, 1854.

2. When we were the political slaves of King George, and wanted to be free, we called the maxim that "all men are created equal" a self-evident truth, but now when we have grown fat, and have lost all dread of being slaves ourselves, we have become so greedy to be masters that we call the same maxim "a self-evident lie." The Fourth of July has not quite dwindled away; it is still a great day—for burning firecrackers!—*Letter to G. Robertson*, August 15, 1855.

3. As a nation we began by declaring that "all men are created equal." We now practically read it "all men are created equal, except negroes." When the Know-nothings get control, it will read "all men are created equal, except negroes and foreigners and Catholics." When it comes to this, I shall prefer emigrating to some country where they make no pretense of loving liberty—to Russia, for instance, where despotism can be taken pure, and without the base alloy of hypocrisy.—*Letter to J. F. Speed*, August 24, 1855.

4. I think the authors of that notable instrument [Declaration of Independence] intended to include *all* men, but they did not intend to declare all men equal *in all respects.* They did not mean to say all were equal in color, size, intellect, moral development, or social capacity. They defined with tolerable distinctness in what respects they did consider all men created equal—equal with "certain inalienable rights, among which are life, liberty, and the pursuit of happiness." This they said, and this they meant. They did not mean to assert the obvious untruth that all were then actually enjoying that equality, nor yet that they were about to confer it immediately upon them. In fact, they had no power to confer such a boon. They meant simply to declare the right, so that enforcement of it might follow as fast as circumstances should permit. They meant to set up a standard maxim for free society, which should be familiar to all, and revered by all; constantly looked to, constantly labored for, and even though never perfectly attained, constantly approximated, and thereby constantly spreading and deepening in influence and augmenting the happiness and value of life to all people of all colors everywhere.—*Springfield Speech,* June 27, 1857.

5. Let us discard all this quibbling about this man and the other man, this race and that race and the other race being inferior, and therefore they must be placed in an inferior position. Let us discard all these things, and unite as one people throughout this land, until we shall once more stand up declaring that all

men are created equal.—*Chicago Speech,* July 10, 1858.

6. Certainly the Negro is not our equal in color —perhaps not in many other respects; still, in the right to put into his mouth the bread that his own hands have earned he is the equal of every other man, white or black.—*Springfield Speech,* July 17, 1858.

7. Anything that argues me into the idea of perfect social and political equality with the negro is but a specious and fantastic arrangement of words, by which a man can prove a horsechestnut to be a chestnut horse. . . . I have no purpose to introduce political and social equality between the white and the black races. There is a physical difference between the two, which, in my judgment, will probably forever forbid their living together upon the footing of perfect equality. . . . I have never said anything to the contrary, but I hold that, notwithstanding all this, there is no reason in the world why the negro is not entitled to all the natural rights enumerated in the Declaration of Independence—the right to life, liberty, and the pursuit of happiness. I hold that he is as much entitled to these as the white man.—*Reply at Ottawa Debate,* August 21, 1858.

SEE ALSO: Liberty 7; Negroes 1; Revolution 1.

ERROR

1. I cannot claim that I am entirely free from all error in the opinions I advance.—*Speech at Galesburg Debate,* October 7, 1858.

2. I shall try to correct errors when shown to be

errors, and I shall adopt new views so fast as they shall appear to be true views.—*Open Letter to H. Greeley,* August 22, 1862.

3. I frequently make mistakes myself in the many things I am compelled to do hastily.—*To General W. S. Rosecrans,* May 20, 1863.

SEE ALSO: God 5; Opinion 1.

EVENTS

I claim not to have controlled events, but confess plainly that events have controlled me.—*Letter to A. G. Hodges,* April 4, 1864.

SEE ALSO: Death 1; Progress 2.

EXPERIENCE

1. We know nothing of what will happen in future, but by the analogy of past experience.—*Speech on Subtreasury,* December 20, 1839.

2. We dare not disregard the lessons of experience.—*Letter to J. M. Clayton,* July 28, 1849.

SEE ALSO: Knowledge; Morals; Negroes 5.

– F –

FALSEHOOD

I believe it is an established maxim in morals that he who makes an assertion without knowing whether it is true or false is guilty of falsehood, and the accidental truth of the assertion does not justify or excuse him.—*Letter to Editor of Illinois Gazette,* August 11, 1846.

FASHION

It is said by some that men will think and act for themselves; that none will disuse spirits or anything else because his neighbors do; and that moral influence is not that powerful engine contended for. Let us examine this. Let me ask the man who could maintain this position most stiffly, what compensation he will accept to go to church some Sunday and sit during the sermon with his wife's bonnet upon his head? Not a trifle, I'll venture. And why not? There would be nothing irreligious in it, nothing immoral, nothing uncomfortable—then why not? Is it not because there would be something egregiously unfashionable in it? Then it is the influence of fashion; and what is the influence of fashion but the influence that other people's actions have on our actions—the strong inclination each of us feels to do as we see all our neighbors do? Nor is the influence of fashion confined to any particular thing or class of things; it is just as strong on one subject as another.—*Temperance Address,* February 22, 1842.

FORCE

The government will not use force, unless force is used against it.—*Address in Independence Hall,* February 22, 1861.

SEE ALSO: Peace 3; Providence 1; Slavery 9.

FREEDOM

1. Those who deny freedom to others, deserve it not for themselves; and, under the rule of a just God, cannot long retain it.—*The "Lost" Speech at Bloomington,* May 29, 1856.

2. I believe each individual is naturally entitled to do as he pleases with himself and the fruits of his labor, so far as it in no wise interferes with any other man's rights.—*Chicago Speech,* July 10, 1858.

3. I say that there is room enough for us all to be free, and that it not only does not wrong the white man that the negro should be free, but it positively wrongs the mass of the white men that the negro should be enslaved; that the mass of white men are

really injured by the effects of slave-labor in the vicinity of the fields of their own labor.—*Speech at Cincinnati,* September 17, 1859.

4. In giving freedom to the slave, we assure freedom to the free.—*Annual Message to Congress,* December 1, 1862.

5. I have always thought that all men should be free.—*Speech to Indiana Regiment,* March 17, 1865.

SEE ALSO: Abolition 2; Democracy 4; Emancipation 2; Moderation; Negroes 6; Politics 5; Slavery 11.

FRIENDSHIP

1. How miserably things seem to be arranged in this world! If we have no friends, we have no pleasure; and if we have them, we are sure to lose them, and be doubly pained by the loss.—*Letter to J. F. Speed,* February 25, 1842.

2. The better part of one's life consists in his friendships.—*Letter to J. Gillespie,* May 19, 1849.

3. The loss of enemies does not compensate for the loss of friends.—*Telegram to Secretary W. H. Seward,* June 30, 1862.

SEE ALSO: Conscience 2; Persuasion.

– G –

GENIUS

Towering genius disdains a beaten path. It seeks regions hitherto unexplored. It sees no distinction in adding story to story upon the monuments of fame erected to the memory of others. It denies that it is glory enough to serve under any chief. It scorns to tread in the footsteps of any predecessor, however illustrious.—*Lyceum Address,* January 27, 1837.

GOD

1. In great contests each party claims to act in accordance with the will of God. Both may be, and one must be, wrong. God cannot be for and against the same thing at the same time.—*From a recorded Meditation,* September 30, 1862.

2. I am concerned to know, not whether the Lord is on my side, but whether I am on the Lord's side.—*Remark as quoted in I. M. Tarbell's Life of Abraham Lincoln, II,* 92.

3. Let us diligently apply the means, never doubt-

ing that a just God, in His own good time, will give us the rightful result.—*Letter to J. C. Conkling,* August 26, 1863.

4. If we do right God will be with us, and if God is with us we cannot fail.—*Proclamation for a Day of Prayer,* July 7, 1864.

5. The purposes of the Almighty are perfect, and must prevail, though we erring mortals may fail to accurately perceive them in advance. We hoped for a happy termination of this terrible war long before this; but God knows best, and has ruled otherwise. We shall yet acknowledge His wisdom, and our own error therein. Meanwhile we must work earnestly in the best lights He gives us, trusting that so working still conduces to the great ends He ordains. Surely, He intends some great good to follow this mighty convulsion, which no mortal could make, and no mortal could stay.—*Letter to Mrs. E. Gurney,* September 4, 1864.

SEE ALSO: Atheism; Bible; Charity; Freedom 1; Personal Worth; Prayer; Religion 1; Thanksgiving.

GOOD AND EVIL

1. The true rule, in determining to embrace or reject anything, is not whether it have any evil in it, but whether it have more of evil than of good. There are few things wholly evil or wholly good. Almost everything, especially of government policy, is an inseparable compound of the two; so that our best judgment of the preponderance between them is con-

41

tinually demanded.—*Speech on Internal Improvements,* July 20, 1848.

2. I hold that while man exists it is his duty to improve not only his own condition, but to assist in ameliorating mankind; and therefore, without entering upon the details of the question, I will simply say that I am for those means which will give the greatest good to the greatest number.—*Address to Cincinnati Germans,* February 12, 1861.

SEE ALSO: Progress 3; Temperance 5.

GOVERNMENT

1. That our government should have been maintained in its original form, from its establishment until now, is not much to be wondered at. It had many props to support it through that period, which are now decayed and crumbled away. Through that period it was felt by all to be an undecided experiment, now it is understood to be a successful one. Then all that sought celebrity and fame and distinction expected to find them in the success of that experiment. Their all was staked upon it; their destiny was inseparably linked with it. Their ambition aspired to display before an admiring world a practical demonstration of the truth which had hitherto been considered at best no better than problematical—namely, the capability of a people to govern themselves.—*Lyceum Address,* January 27, 1837.

2. Why . . . should we have government? Why not each individual take to himself the whole fruit of

his labor, without having any of it taxed away, in services, corn or money? Why not take just so much land as he can cultivate with his own hands, without buying it of anyone? The legitimate object of government is to do for a community of people whatever they need to have done, but cannot do at all, or cannot do so well, for themselves, in their separate and individual capacities. In all that the people can individually do as well for themselves, government ought not to interfere.—*A Fragment on Government*, c. July 1, 1854.

3. Government is a combination of the people of a country to effect certain objects by joint effort.—*A Fragment on Government*, c. July 1, 1854.

4. No man is good enough to govern another man without that other's consent.—*Speech at Peoria*, October 16, 1854.

5. I believe this government cannot endure permanently half slave and half free. I do not expect the Union to be dissolved—I do not expect the house to fall—but I do expect it will cease to be divided. It will become all one thing, or all the other. Either the opponents of slavery will arrest the further spread of it, and place it where the public mind shall rest in the belief that it is in the course of ultimate extinction; or its advocates will push it forward till it shall become alike lawful in all the States, old as well as new, North as well as South.—*Springfield Speech*, June 16, 1858.

6. It is no function of government to prohibit what

is not wrong.—*Speeches at Kansas*, December 1-5, 1859.

7. While the people retain their virtue and vigilance, no administration, by any extreme of wickedness or folly, can very seriously injure the government in the short space of four years.—*First Inaugural Address*, March 4, 1861.

8. No government proper ever had a provision in its organic law for its own termination.—*A Message to Congress*, July 4, 1861.

9. Let the friends of the government first save the government and then administer it to their own liking.—*Letter to H. W. Davis*, March 18, 1863.

10. It is said that we have the best government the world ever knew, and I am glad to meet you, the supporters of that government.—*Speech to 189th New York Regiment*, October 24, 1864.

11. We cannot have free government without elections.—*Response to a Serenade*, November 10, 1864.

SEE ALSO: Borrowing; Capital; Church 1; Democracy 4; Equality 1; Justice 4; Mob Law 1; Money 5; Peace 2; Public Opinion 2; Self-government; Sovereignty 2; Supreme Court; Tariff.

– H –

HISTORY

1. I do not mean to say that the scenes of the Revolution are now or ever will be entirely forgotten, but that, like everything else, they must fade upon the memory of the world, and grow more and more dim by the lapse of time. In history, we hope, they will be read of, and recounted, so long as the Bible shall be read; but even granting that they will, their influence cannot be what it heretofore has been. Even then they cannot be so universally known nor so vividly felt as they were by the generation just gone to rest. . . .

Those histories are gone. They can be read no more forever. They were a fortress of strength; but what invading foeman could never do, the silent artillery of time has done—the leveling of its walls. They are gone. They were a forest of giant oaks; but the all-resistless hurricane has swept over them, and left only here and there a lonely trunk, despoiled of its verdure, shorn of its foliage, unshading and unshaded, to murmur in a few more gentle breezes, and to combat with its mutilated limbs a few more ruder storms, then to sink and be no more.

They were pillars of the temple of liberty; and now that they have crumbled away that temple must fall unless we, their descendants, supply their places with other pillars, hewn from the solid quarry of sober reason. Passion has helped us, but can do so no more. It will in future be our enemy. Reason—cold, calculating, unimpassioned reason—must furnish all the materials for our future support and defense. Let those materials be molded into general intelligence, sound morality, and, in particular, a reverence for the Constitution and laws; and that we improved to the last, that we remained free to the last.—*Lyceum Address,* January 27, 1837.

2. What has once happened will invariably happen again when the same circumstances which combined to produce it shall again combine in the same way.—*Speech on Subtreasury,* December 20, 1839.

3. History is not history unless it is the truth.—*Letter to W. H. Herndon,* 1856.

4. We cannot escape history. We of this Congress and this administration will be remembered in spite of ourselves. No personal significance or insignificance can spare one or another of us. The fiery trial through which we pass will light us down in honor or dishonor to the latest generation.—*Annual Message to Congress,* December 1, 1862.

SEE ALSO: Ambition 2.

HOPE

1. Free labor has the inspiration of hope; pure slavery has no hope. The power of hope upon human exertion and happiness is wonderful. The slave-master himself has a conception of it, and hence the system of tasks among slaves. The slave whom you cannot drive with the lash to break seventy-five pounds of hemp in a day, if you will task him to break a hundred, and promise him pay for all he does over, he will break you a hundred and fifty. You have substituted hope for the rod. And yet perhaps it does not occur to you that to the extent of your gain in the case, you have given up the slave system of labor. —*A Fragment on Slavery*, c. July 1, 1854.

2. No oppressed people will fight, and endure, as our fathers did, without the promise of something better than a mere change of masters.—*From an undated Fragment*, c. 1860.

SEE ALSO: Declaration of Independence 3; Justice 3; War 5.

HUMAN NATURE

1. Human action can be modified to some extent, but human nature cannot be changed.—*Address at Cooper Institute*, February 27, 1860.

2. Human nature is the same—people at the South are the same as those at the North, barring the differences in circumstances.—*Hartford Speech*, March 5, 1860.

SEE ALSO: Cause and Effect.

– I –

IDLENESS

1. Universal idleness would speedily result in universal ruin.—*Tariff Memorandum,* December 1, 1847.

2. No country can sustain in idleness more than a small percentage of its numbers. The great majority must labor at something productive.—*Address before the Wisconsin State Agricultural Society,* September 30, 1859.

IMMIGRANTS

1. In regard to . . . foreigners, I esteem them no better than other people, nor any worse. It is not my nature, when I see a people borne down by the weight of their shackles—the oppression of tyranny—to make their life more bitter by heaping upon them greater burdens; but rather would I do all in my power to raise the yoke than to add anything that would tend to crush them. In as much as our country is extensive and new, and the countries of Europe are densely populated, if there are any abroad who desire to make

48

this the land of their adoption, it is not in any heart to throw aught in their way to prevent them from coming to the United States.—*Address to Germans in Cincinnati,* February 12, 1861.

2. It is the duty of all aliens residing in the United States to submit to and obey the laws, and respect authority of the government . . . They cannot be required to take an oath of allegiance to this government, because it conflicts with the duty they owe to their own sovereigns.—*Military Order,* July 22, 1862.

3. I regard our immigrants as one of the principal replenishing streams which are appointed by Providence to repair the ravages of internal war, and its wastes of national strength and health. All that is necessary is to secure the flow of that stream in its present fullness, and to that end the government must, in every way, make it manifest that it neither needs nor designs to impose involuntary military service upon those who come from other lands to cast their lot in our country.—*Annual Message to Congress,* December 6, 1864.

INVENTION

1. To be fruitful in invention, it is indispensable to have a habit of observation and reflection; and this habit our steam friend acquired, no doubt, from those who, to him, were old fogies.—*Lecture on "Discoveries, Inventions, and Improvements,"* c. February 22, 1859.

2. The successful application of steam power to

farm work is a desideratum—especially a steam-plow. It is not enough that a machine operated by steam will really plow. To be successful, it must, all things considered, plow better than can be done with animal power. It must do all the work as well, and cheaper or more rapidly, so as to get through more perfectly in season; or in some way afford an advantage over plowing with animals, else it is no success. I have never seen a machine intended for a steam-plow. Much praise and admiration are bestowed upon some of them; and they may be, for aught I know, already successful; but I have not perceived the demonstration of it. I have thought a good deal, in an abstract way, about a steam-plow. That one which shall be so contrived as to apply the larger proportion of its power to the cutting and turning of the soil, and the smallest to the moving itself over the field, will be the best one. A very small stationary engine would draw a large gang of plows through the ground from a short distance to itself; but when it is not stationary, but has to move along like a horse, dragging the plows after it, it must have additional power to carry itself; and the difficulty grows by what is intended to overcome it; for what adds power, also adds size and weight to the machine, thus increasing again the demand for power. Suppose you should construct the machine so as to cut a succession of short furrows, say a rod in length, traversely to the course the machine is locomoting, something like the shuttle in weaving. In such case the whole machine would move north only the width of a furrow, while in length the furrow would be a rod from east to west. In such case a very large proportion of the power would be applied to the actual plowing. But in this, too, there would be a difficulty, which would be the getting of the plow into and out of the ground at the ends of all these short furrows.

I believe, however, ingenious men will, if they have not already, overcome the difficulties I have suggested.—*Address before the Wisconsin State Agricultural Society,* September 30, 1859.

SEE ALSO: Printing; Speech; Writing.

– J –

JUDICIAL DECISIONS

Judicial decisions have two uses—first, to absolutely determine the case decided; and secondly, to indicate to the public how other similar cases will be decided when they arise. For the latter use, they are called "precedents."—*Springfield Speech,* June 26, 1857.

SEE ALSO: Public Opinion 3; Supreme Court.

JUSTICE

1. My faith in the proposition that each man should do precisely as he pleases with all which is exclusively his own lies at the foundation of the sense of justice there is in me. I extend the principle to communities of men as well as to individuals. I so extend it because it is politically wise, as well as naturally just.—*Speech at Peoria,* October 16, 1854.

2. Your hisses will not blow down the walls of justice.—*Speech at Cincinnati,* September 17, 1859.

3. Why should there not be a patient confidence in the ultimate justice of the people? Is there any

better or equal hope in the world? In our present differences, is either party without faith of being in the right? If the Almighty Ruler of the nations, with His eternal truth and justice, be on your side of the North, or on your side of the South, that truth and that justice will surely prevail by the judgment of this great tribunal of the American people.—*First Inaugural Adress,* March 4, 1861.

4. It is as much the duty of government to render prompt justice against itself, in favor of citizens, as it is to administer the same between private individuals.—*Annual Message to Congress,* December 3, 1861.

5. The severest justice may not always be the best policy.—*Message to Congress,* July 17, 1862.

SEE ALSO: Conduct 3; Law 6, 8; Office Seekers 1; Party 2; Slavery 3, 6.

– K –

KNOWLEDGE
He who affirms what he does not know to be true falsifies as much as he who affirms what he does not know to be false.—*Notes for Speeches,* c. October 1, 1858.

SEE ALSO: Falsehood.

— L —

LABOR

1. In the early days of our race the Almighty said to the first of our race, "In the sweat of thy face shalt thou eat bread"; and since then, if we except the light and the air of heaven, no good thing has been or can be enjoyed by us without having first cost labor. And inasmuch as most good things are produced by labor, it follows that all such things of right belong to those whose labor has produced them. But it has so happened, in all ages of the world, that some have labored, and others have without labor enjoyed a large proportion of the fruits. This is wrong, and should not continue. To secure to each laborer the whole product of his labor, or as nearly as possible, is a worthy object of any good government.—*Temperance Address*, February 22, 1842.

2. As labor is the common burden of our race, so the effort of some to shift their share of the burden on the shoulders of others is the greatest durable curse of the race.—*A Fragment on Slavery*, c. July 1, 1854.

3. They [Southerners] think that men are always to remain as laborers here—but there is no such class. The man who labored for another last year, this year labors for himself, and next year will hire others to labor for him.—*Speech at Kalamazoo,* August 27, 1856.

4. Labor is the great source from which nearly all, if not all, human comforts and necessities are drawn. There is a difference in opinion about the elements of labor in society. Some men assume that there is a necessary connection between capital and labor, and that connection draws within it the whole of the labor of the community. They assume that nobody works unless capital excites them to work. They begin next to consider what is the best way. They say there are but two ways—one is to hire men and to allure them to labor by their consent; the other is to buy the men and drive them to it, and that is slavery. Having assumed that, they proceed to discuss the question of whether the laborers themselves are better off in the condition of slaves or of hired laborers, and they usually decide that they are better off in the condition of slaves.

In the first place, I say that the whole thing is a mistake. That there is a certain relation between capital and labor, I admit. That it does exist, and rightfully exists, I think is true. That men who are industrious and sober and honest in the pursuit of their own interests should after a while accumulate capital, and after that should be allowed to enjoy it in peace, and also if they should choose, when they have accumulated it, to use it to save themselves from actual labor, and hire other people to labor for them, is right. In doing so, they do not wrong the man they employ, for they find men who have not their own land to work upon, or shops to work in, and who are benefited by working for others—hired laborers, receiving their capital for it. Thus a few men that own capital hire a few others, and these establish the relation of capital and labor rightfully—a relation of which I make no complaint.—*Speech at Cincinnati,* September 17, 1859.

5. The world is agreed that labor is the source from which human wants are mainly supplied. There is no dispute upon that point. From this point, however, men immediately diverge. Much disputation is maintained as to the best way of applying and controlling the labor element. By some it is assumed that labor is available only in connection with capital— that nobody labors, unless somebody else owning capital, somehow, by the use of it, induces him to do it. Having assumed this, they proceed to consider whether it is best that capital shall hire laborers, and thus induce them to work by their own consent, or buy them, and drive them to it, without their consent. Having proceeded so far, they naturally conclude that all laborers are naturally either hired laborers or slaves. They further assume that whoever is once a hired laborer, is fatally fixed in that condition for life; and thence again, that his condition is as bad as, or worse than, that of a slave. This is the "mud-sill"

theory. But another class of reasoners hold the opinion that there is no such relation between capital and labor as assumed; that there is no such thing as a free man being fatally fixed for life in the condition of a hired laborer; that both these assumptions are false, and all inferences from them groundless. They hold that labor is prior to, and independent of, capital; that, in fact, capital is the fruit of labor, and could never have existed if labor had not first existed; that labor can exist without capital, but that capital could never have existed without labor. Hence they hold that labor is the superior—greatly the superior—of capital.

They do not deny that there is, and probably always will be, a relation between labor and capital. The error, as they hold, is in assuming that the whole labor of the world exists within that relation. A few men own capital, and that few avoid labor themselves, and with their capital hire or buy another few to labor for them. A large majority belong to neither class—neither work for others, nor have others working for them . . . Men, with their families—wives, sons and daughters—work for themselves, on their farms, in their houses, and in their shops, taking the whole product to themselves, and asking no favors of capital on the one hand, nor of hirelings or slaves on the other. It is not forgotten that a considerable number of persons mingle their own labor with capital—that is, labor with their own hands and also buy slaves or hire free men to labor for them; but this is only a mixed, and not a distinct class. No principle stated is disturbed by the existence of this mixed class. Again, as has already been said, the opponents of the "mud-sill" theory insist that there is not, of necessity, any such thing as the free hired labor being fixed to that condition for life. There is demonstration for saying this. Many independent men in this assembly doubtless a few years ago were hired laborers. And their case is almost, if not quite, the general rule.— *Address before the Wisconsin State Agricultural Society,* September 30, 1859.

6. The prudent penniless beginner in the world labors for wages for a while, saves a surplus with which to buy tools or land for himself, then labors on his own account for another while, and at length hires another new beginner to help him. This . . . is free labor—the just and generous and prosperous system which opens the way for all—gives hope to all, and energy, and progress, and improvement of condition to all. If any continue through life in the condition of the hired laborer, it is not the fault of the system, but because of either a dependent nature which prefers it, or improvidence, folly, or singular misfortune. —*Address before the Wisconsin State Agricultural Society,* September 30, 1859.

7. I am glad to see that a system of labor prevails in New England under which laborers can strike when they want to . . . I like the system which lets

a man quit when he wants to, and wish it might prevail everywhere.—*New Haven Speech*, March 6, 1860.

8. Labor is like any other commodity in the market—increase the demand for it and you increase the price for it.—*Annual Message to Congress*, December 1, 1862.

SEE ALSO: Capital; Education 2; Emancipation 2; Hope 1; Property 3; Tariff.

LAND

1. Part with the land you have, and, my life upon it, you will never after own a spot big enough to bury you in.—*Letter to J. D. Johnston*, November 4, 1851.

2. In so far as the government lands can be disposed of, I am in favor of cutting up the wild lands into parcels, so that every poor man may have a home. —*Address to Germans at Cincinnati*, February 12, 1861.

SEE ALSO: Government 2; Invention 2.

LAW

1. With regard to existing laws, some alterations are thought to be necessary. Many respectable men have suggested that our estray laws, the law respecting the issuing of executions, the road law, and some others, are deficient in their present form, and require alterations. But, considering the great probability that the framers of those laws were wiser than myself, I should prefer not meddling with them, unless

they were first attacked by others.—*Address to the People of Sangamon County,* March 9, 1832.

2. Although bad laws, if they exist, should be repealed as soon as possible, still, while they continue in force, for the sake of example they should be religiously observed. So also in unprovided cases. If such arise, let proper legal provisions be made for them with the least possible delay, but till then let them, if not too intolerable, be borne with.—*Lyceum Address,* January 27, 1837.

3. Let every man remember that to violate the law is to trample on the blood of his father, and to tear the charter of his own and his children's liberty. Let reverence for the laws be breathed by every American mother to the lisping babe that prattles on her lap; let it be taught in schools, in seminaries, and in colleges; let it be written in primers, spelling-books, and in almanacs; let it be preached from the pulpit, proclaimed in legislative halls, and enforced in courts of justice. And, in short, let it become the political religion of the nation; and let the old and the young, the rich and poor, the grave and the gay of all sexes and tongues and colors and conditions, sacrifice unceasingly upon its altars.—*Lyceum Address,* January 27, 1837.

4. No law is stronger than the public sentiment where it is to be enforced.—*Letter to J. J. Crittenden,* 1859.

5. The intention of the lawgiver is the law.—*First Inaugural Address,* March 4, 1861.

6. Nothing should ever be implied as law which leads to unjust or absurd consequences.—*Message to Congress,* July 4, 1861.

7. Necessity knows no law.—*Telegram to Governor Ramsey,* August 27, 1862.

8. A law may be both constitutional and expedient, and yet may be administered in an unjust and unfair way.—*Opinion on the Darft,* c. August 15, 1863. unfair way.—*Opinion on the Draft,* c. August 15, 1863.

SEE ALSO: Conduct 7; Government 8; Immigrants 2; Lawyers; Mob Law 1, 2; Nation 2; People 6; Right and Wrong 2; Slavery 5.

LAWYERS

There is a vague popular belief that lawyers are necessarily dishonest. I say vague, because when we consider to what extent confidence and honors are reposed in and conferred upon lawyers by the people, it appears improbable that their impression of dishonesty is very distinct and vivid. Yet the impression is common, almost universal. Let no young man choosing the law for a calling for a moment yield to the popular belief—resolve to be honest at all events; and if in your own judgment you cannot be an honest lawyer, resolve to be honest without being a lawyer. Choose some other occupation, rather than one in the choosing of which you do, in advance, consent to be a knave.—*Notes for Law Lecture,* c. July 1, 1850.

SEE ALSO: Diligence; Litigation; Temperance 1.

LEADERSHIP

1. Some single mind must be master, else there will be no agreement in anything.—*A Remark, as quoted in Nicolay and Hay, History, VIII, 416,* c. February 17, 1863.

2. As a pilot I have used my best exertions to keep afloat our Ship of State, and shall be glad to resign my trust at the appointed time to another pilot more skillful and successful than I may prove.—*Reply to Presbyterian General Assembly,* May 30, 1863.

SEE ALSO: Man.

LIBERTY

1. Let North and South—let all Americans—let all lovers of liberty everywhere join in the great and good work. If we do this, we shall not only have saved the Union, but we shall have so saved it as to make and to keep it forever worthy of the saving. We shall have so saved it that the succeeding millions of free, happy people, the world over, shall rise up and call us blessed to the latest generations.—*Speech at Peoria,* October 16, 1854.

2. We must make this a land of liberty in fact, as it is in name. But in seeking to attain these results—so indispensable if the liberty which is our pride and boast shall endure—we will be loyal to the Constitution and to the "flag of our Union," and no matter what our grievance . . . we will say to the Southern disunionists, *we* won't go out of the Union, and *you* SHAN'T!—*The "Lost" Speech at Bloomington,* May 29, 1856.

3. In their enlightened belief, nothing stamped with the divine image and likeness was sent into the world to be trodden on and degraded and imbruted by its fellows. They [the men responsible for the Declaration of Independence] grasped not only the whole race of man then living, but they reached forward and seized upon the farthest posterity. They erected a beacon to guide their children and their children's children, and the countless myriads who should inhabit the earth in other ages. Wise statesmen as they were, they knew the tendency of prosperity to breed tyrants, and so they established these great self-evident truths, that when, in the distant future, some man, some faction, some interest, should set up the doctrine that none but rich men, none but white men, or none but Anglo-Saxon white men were entitled to life, liberty, and the pursuit of happiness, their posterity might look up again to the Declaration of Independence and take courage to renew the battle which their fathers began, so that truth and justice and mercy and all the humane and Christian virtues might not be extinguished from the land; so that no man would hereafter dare to limit and circumscribe the great principles on which the temple of liberty was being built.—*Speech at Lewiston,* August 17, 1858.

4. What constitutes the bulwark of our own liberty and independence? It is not our frowning battlements, our bristling sea coasts, our army and our navy. These are not our reliance against tyranny. All of these may be turned against us without making us

64

weaker for the struggle. Our reliance is in the love of liberty which God has planted in us. Our defense is in the spirit which prized liberty as the heritage of all men, in all lands everywhere. Destroy this spirit and you have planted the seeds of despotism at your own doors. Familiarize yourselves with the chains of bondage and you prepare your own limbs to wear them. Accustomed to trample on the rights of others, you have lost the genius of your own independence and become the fit subjects of the first cunning tyrant who rises among you.—*Speech at Edwardsville,* September 13, 1858.

5. The fight must go on. The cause of civil liberty must not be surrendered at the end of one or even one hundred defeats.—*Letter to H. Asbury,* November 19, 1858.

6. We all declare for liberty; but in using the same word we do not all mean the same thing. With some the word liberty may mean for each man to do as he pleases with himself, and the product of his labor; while with others the same word may mean for some men to do as they please with other men, and the product of other men's labor. Here are two, not only different, but incompatible things, called by the same name, liberty . . . The shepherd drives the wolf from the sheep's throat, for which the sheep thanks the shepherd as his liberator, while the wolf denounces him for the same act, as destroyer of liberty, especially as the sheep was a black one. Plainly, the sheep and the wolf are not agreed upon a definition

65

of the word liberty; and precisely the same difference prevails today among us, human creatures, even in the North, and all professing to love liberty.—*Address at Sanitary Fair,* April 18, 1864.

7. Nowhere in the world is presented a government of so much liberty and equality. To the humblest and poorest amongst us are held out the highest privileges and positions. The present moment finds me at the White House, yet there is as good a chance for your children as there was for my father's.—*Speech to 148th Ohio Regiment,* August 31, 1864.

SEE ALSO: Constitution 2; Democracy 3; Duty 1; Prosperity 1; Self-government 3.

LIFE

By general law, life and limb must be protected, yet often a limb must be amputated to save a life; but a life is never wisely given to save a limb.—*Letter to A. G. Hodges,* April 4, 1864.

SEE ALSO: Friendship 2; Soldiers.

LIQUOR

I have not inquired at what period of time the use of intoxicating liquors commenced; nor is it important to know. It is sufficient that to all of us who now inhabit the world, the practice of drinking them is just as old as the world itself—that is, we have seen the one just as long as we have seen the other. When all such of us as have now reached the years of maturity first opened our eyes upon the stage of existence, we found intoxicating liquor recognized by everybody, used by everybody, repudiated by nobody. It commonly entered into the first draught of the infant and the last draught of the dying man. From the sideboard of the parson down to the ragged pocket of the houseless loafer, it was constantly found. Physicians prescribed it in this, that, and the other disease; government provided it for soldiers and sailors; and to have a rolling or raising, a husking or "hoedown," anywhere about without it was positively insufferable. So, too, it was everywhere a respectable article of manufacture and merchandise. The making of it was regarded as an honorable livelihood, and he who could make most was the most enterprising and respectable. Large and small manufactories of it were everywhere erected, in which all the earthly goods of their owners were invested. Wagons drew it from town to town; boats bore it from clime to clime, and the winds wafted it from nation to nation; and merchants bought and sold it, by wholesale and retail, with precisely the same feelings on the part of the seller, buyer, and bystander as are felt at the selling and buying of plows, beef, bacon, or any other of the real necessaries of life. Universal public opinion not only tolerated but recognized and adopted its use.

It is true that even then it was known and acknowledged that many were greatly injured by it; but none seemed to think the injury arose from the use of a bad thing, but from the abuse of a very good thing. The victims of it were to be pitied and compassioned, just as are the heirs of consumption and other hereditary diseases. Their failing was treated as a misfortune, and not as a crime, or even as a disgrace. If, then, what I have been saying is true, is it wonderful that some should think and act now as all thought and acted twenty years ago? and is it just to assail, condemn, or despise them for doing so?—*Temperance Address*, February 22, 1842.

SEE ALSO: Temperance.

LITIGATION

Discourage litigation. Persuade neighbors to compromise whenever you can. Point out to them how the nominal winner is often a real loser—in fees, expenses, and waste of time. As a peacemaker the lawyer has a superior opportunity of being a good man. There will still be business enough.

Never stir up litigation. A worse man can scarcely be found than one who does this. Who can be more nearly a fiend than he who habitually overhauls the register of deeds in search of defects in titles, whereon to stir up strife and put money in his pocket? A moral tone ought to be infused into the profession which should drive such men out of it.—*Notes for Law Lecture*, c. July 1, 1850.

LOGIC

If a man will stand up and assert, and repeat and re-assert, that two and two do not make four, I know nothing in the power of argument that can stop him.

I think I can answer the judge so long as he sticks to the premises; but when he flies from them, I cannot work any argument into the consistency of a mental gag and actually close his mouth with it.—*Speech at Peoria,* October 16, 1854.

SEE ALSO: Reason 3.

LOYALTY

1. Many free countries have lost their liberty, and ours may lose hers; but if she shall, be it my proudest plume, not that I was the last to desert, but that I never deserted her.—*Speech on Subtreasury,* December 20, 1839.

2. I have found that men who have not even been suspected of disloyalty are very averse to taking an oath of any sort as a condition to exercising an ordinary right of citizenship.—*Letter to General W. S. Rosecrans,* April 4, 1863.

SEE ALSO: Patriotism 4.

– M –

MAJORITY

1. If the majority should not rule, who would be the judge? Where is such a judge to be found? We should all be bound by the majority of the American people; if not, then the minority must control. Would that be right? Would it be just or generous? Assuredly not. I reiterate that the majority should rule.—*Address at Steubenville*, February 14, 1861.

2. A majority held in restraint by constitutional checks and limitations, and always changing easily with deliberate changes of popular opinions and sentiments, is the only true sovereign of a free people. Whoever rejects it does, of necessity, fly to anarchy or to despotism. Unanimity is impossible; the rule of a minority, as a permanent arrangement, is wholly inadmissible; so that, rejecting the majority principle, anarchy or despotism in some form is all that is left. —*First Inaugural Address*, March 4, 1861.

3. If by the mere force of numbers a majority should deprive a minority of any clearly written con-

stitutional right, it might in a moral point of view justify revolution—certianly would if such a right were a vital one.—*A Message to Congress,* July 4, 1861.

4. In a great national crisis like ours, unanimity of action among those seeking a common end is very desirable—almost indispensable. And yet no approach to such unanimity is attainable unless some deference shall be paid to the will of the majority, simply because it is the will of the majority.—*Annual Message to Congress,* December 4, 1864.

SEE ALSO: Idleness 2; Revolution 2, 3.

MALICE

1. I shall do nothing in malice. What I deal with is too vast for malicious dealing.—*Letter to C. Bullitt,* July 28, 1862.

2. With malice toward none, with charity for all, with firmness in the right as God gives us to see the right, let us strive on to finish the work we are in, to bind up the nation's wounds, to care for him who shall have borne the battle and for his widow and his orphan, to do all which may achieve and cherish a just and lasting peace among ourselves and with all nations.—*Second Inaugural Address,* March 4, 1865.

SEE ALSO: Civil War 2.

MAN

Assume to dictate to man's judgment, or to command his action or to mark him out as one to be shunned and despised, and he will retreat within himself, close all the avenues to his head and heart; and though your cause be naked truth itself, transformed to the heaviest lance, harder than steel and sharper than steel can be made, and though you throw it with more than herculean force and decision, you will be no more able to pierce him than to penetrate the hard shell of a tortoise with a rye straw. Such is man and so must he be understood by those who would lead him even to his own best interests.—*Temperance Address,* February 22, 1842.

SEE ALSO: Education 2.

MARRIAGE

1. I protest, now and forever, against that counterfeit logic which presumes that because I do not want a negro woman for a slave, I do necessarily want her for a wife. My understanding is that I need not have her for either; but, as God made us separate, we can leave one another alone, and do one another much good thereby. There are white men enough to marry all the white women, and enough black men to marry all the black women, and in God's name let them be so married.—*Chicago Speech,* July 10, 1858.

2. In the course of his sermon, [the preacher] asserted that the Savior was the only perfect man who had ever appeared in this world; also, that there was no record in the Bible, or elsewhere, of any perfect woman having lived on the earth. Whereupon there arose in the rear of the church a persecuted-looking

72

personage who, the parson having stopped speaking, said, "*I* know a perfect woman, and for the last six years." "Who was she?" asked the minister. "My husband's first wife," replied the afflicted female.—*Related by C. Sandburg in his War Years, IV, p. 118.*

MEANING

Solomon says there is "a time to keep silence," and when men wrangle by the month with no certainty that they mean the same thing, while using the same word, it perhaps were as well if they would keep silence. The words "coercion" and "invasion" are much used in these days, and often with some temper and hot blood. Let us make sure, if we can, that we do not misunderstand the meaning of those who use them. Let us get exact definitions of these words, not from dictionaries, but from the men themselves, who certainly deprecate the things they would represent by the use of words.—*Address to the Indiana Legislature,* February 12, 1861.

SEE ALSO: Liberty 6.

MINING

1. All creation is a mine, and every man a miner. The whole earth, and all within it, upon it, and round it, including himself, in his physical, moral and intellectual nature, and his susceptibilities, are the infinitely various "leads," from which man, from the first, was to dig out his destiny. In the beginning the

mine was unopened, and the miner stood naked and knowledgeless upon it.—*Lecture on "Discoveries, Inventions, and Improvements,"* February 22, 1859.

2. The immense natural resources of some of these territories ought to be developed as rapidly as possible. Every step in that direction would have a tendency to improve the revenues of the government, and diminish the burdens of the people.—*Annual Message to Congress,* December 1, 1862.

3. I want you to take a message from me to the miners whom you visit. I have very large ideas of the mineral wealth of our nation. I believe it practically inexhaustible. It abounds all over the western country—from the Rocky Mountains to the Pacific, and its development has scarcely commenced. During the war, when we were adding a couple of millions of dollars every day to our national debt, I did not care about encouraging the increase in the volume of our precious metals. We had the country to save first. But now that the rebellion is overthrown, and we know pretty nearly the amount of our national debt, the more gold and silver we mine makes the payment of that debt so much the easier. Now I am going to encourage that in every possible way. We shall have hundreds of thousands of disabled soldiers, and many have feared that their return home in such great numbers might paralyze industry by furnishing suddenly a greater supply of labor than there will be a demand for. I am going to try to attract them to the hidden wealth of our mountain ranges, where there

is room enough for all.—*Letter to S. Colfax,* April 14, 1865.

SEE ALSO: Civil War 4; Thanksgiving.

MISREPRESENTATION

1. When a man hears himself somewhat misrepresented, it provokes him—at least, I find it so with myself; but when misrepresentation becomes very gross and palpable, it is more apt to amuse him.— *Reply at Ottawa Debate,* August 21, 1858.

2. I have found that it is not entirely safe, when one is misrepresented under his very nose, to allow this misrepresentation to go uncontradicted.—*Speech at Columbus,* September 16, 1859.

SEE ALSO: Self-government 3.

MOB LAW

1. When men take it in their heads today to hang gamblers or burn murderers, they should recollect that in the confusion usually attending such transactions they will be as likely to hang or burn some one who is neither a gambler nor a murderer as one who is, and that, acting upon the example they set, the mob of tomorrow may, and probably will, hang or burn some of them by the very same mistake. And not only so; the innocent, those who have ever set their faces against violations of law in every shape, alike with the guilty fall victims to the ravages of mob law; and thus it goes up, step by step, till all the walls erected for the defense of the persons and prop-

75

erty of individuals are trodden down and disregarded. But all this, even, is not the full extent of the evil. By such examples, by instances of the perpetrators of such acts going unpunished, the lawless in spirit are encouraged to become lawless in practice; and having been used to no restraint but dread of punishment, they thus become absolutely unrestrained. Having ever regarded government as their deadliest bane, they make a jubilee of the suspension of its operations, and pray for nothing so much as its total annihilation. While, on the other hand, good men, men who love tranquillity, who desire to abide by the laws and enjoy their benefits, who would gladly spill their blood in the defense of their country, seeing their property destroyed, their families insulted, and their lives endangered, their persons injured, and seeing nothing in prospect that forbodes a change for the better, become tired of and disgusted with a government that offers them no protection, and are not much averse to a change in which they imagine they have nothing to lose. Thus, then, by the operation of this mobocratic spirit which all must admit is now abroad in the land, the strongest bulwark of any government, and particularly of those constituted like ours, may effectually be broken down and destroyed—I mean the attachment of the people. Whenever this effect shall be produced among us; whenever the vicious portion of population shall be permitted to gather in bands of hundreds and thousands, and burn churches, ravage and rob provision-stores, throw printing-presses into rivers, shoot editors, and hang and burn obnoxious persons at pleasure and with impunity, depend on it, this government cannot last. By such things the feelings of the best citizens will become more or less alienated from it, and thus it will be left without friends, or with too few, and those few too weak to make their friendship effectual. At such a time, and under such circumstances, men of sufficient talent and ambition will not be wanting to seize the opportunity, strike the blow, and overturn that fair fabric which for the last half century has been the fondest hope of the lovers of freedom throughout the world.

I know the American people are much attached to their government; I know they would suffer much for its sake; I know they would endure evils long and patiently before they would ever think of exchanging it for another—yet, notwithstanding all this, if the laws be continually despised and disregarded, if their rights to be secure in their persons and property are held by no better tenure than the caprice of a mob, the alienation of their affections from the government is the natural consequence; and to this, sooner or later, it must come.—*Lyceum Address,* January 27, 1837.

2. There is no grievance that is a fit object of redress by mob law. . . . One of two positions is necessarily true—that is, the thing is right within itself, and therefore deserves the protection of all law and all good citizens, or it is wrong, and therefore proper to

be prohibited by legal enactments; and in neither case is the interposition of mob law either necessary, justifiable, or excusable.—*Lyceum Address*, January 27, 1837.

MODERATION

While extremists may find some fault with the moderation of our platform, they should recollect that "the battle is not always to the strong, nor the race to the swift." In grave emergencies, moderation is generally safer than radicalism; and as their struggle is likely to be long and earnest, we must not, by our action, repel any who are in sympathy with us in the main, but rather win all that we can to our standard. We must not belittle nor overlook the facts of our condition—that we are new and comparatively weak, while our enemies are entrenched and relatively strong. They have the administration and the political power; and, right or wrong, at present they have the numbers. Our friends who urge an appeal to arms with so much force and eloquence, should recollect that the government is arrayed against us, and that the numbers are now arrayed against us as well; or, to state it nearer the truth, that they are not yet expressly and affirmatively for us; and that we should repel friends rather than gain them if we adopted anything savoring of revolutionary methods. As it now stands, we must appeal to the sober sense and patriotism of the people. We shall make converts day by day; we shall grow strong by calmness and moderation; we shall grow strong by the violence and injustice of our adversaries. And, unless truth be a mockery and justice a hollow lie, we shall be in the majority after a while, and then the revolution which we shall accomplish will be none the less radical from being the result of pacific measures. The battle of freedom is to be fought out on principle. Slavery is a violation of the eternal right. We have temporized with it from the necessities of our condition; but as sure as God reigns and school children read, *that black foul lie can never be consecrated into God's hallowed truth!—The "Lost" Speech at Bloomington, May 29, 1856.*

MONEY

1. Any person who will reflect that money is only valuable while in circulation, will readily perceive that any device which will keep the government revenues in constant circulation, instead of being locked up in idleness, is no inconsiderable advantage.—*Speech on Subtreasury, December 20, 1839.*

2. No duty is more imperative on that government than the duty it owes the people of furnishing them a sound and uniform currency.—*Speech on Subtreasury, December 20, 1839.*

3. Fluctuations in the value of currency are always injurious, and to reduce these fluctuations to the lowest possible point will always be a leading purpose in wise legislation. Convertibility, prompt and certain convertibility, into coin is generally acknowledged to be the best and surest safeguard against

them.—*Annual Message to Congress,* December 1, 1862.

4. There is powerful temptation in money.—*Letter to W. S. Rosecrans,* March 7, 1863.

5. It seems quite clear that the treasury cannot be successfully conducted unless the government can exercise a restraining power over the bank-note circulation of the country.—*Annual Message to Congress,* December 6, 1864.

SEE ALSO: Litigation; Patriotism 5; Property 2; Punishment.

MORAL CHOICE

The true rule, in determining to embrace or reject anything, is not whether it have any evil in it, but whether it have more of evil than of good. Almost everything, especially of government policy, is an inseparable compound of the two; so that our best judgment of the preponderance between them is continually demanded.—*Speech on Internal Improvements,* June 20, 1848.

MORALS

I believe it is an established maxim in morals that he who makes an assertion without knowing whether it is true or false, is guilty of falsehood.—*Letter to the Editor of the Illinois Gazette,* August 11, 1846.

SEE ALSO: Falsehood; Prosperity 2; Reason 1; Right and Wrong 2, 8.

— N —

NATION

1. Our political problem now is, "Can we as a nation continue together permanently—forever—half slave and half free?" The problem is too mighty for me—may God, in his mercy, superintend the solution. —*Letter to G. Robertson,* August 15, 1855.

2. A nation may be said to consist of its territory, its people, and its laws. The territory is the only part which is of certain durability.—*Annual Message to Congress,* December 1, 1862.

3. Fourscore and seven years ago our fathers brought forth on this continent a new nation, conceived in liberty, and dedicated to the proposition that all men are created equal.—*Gettysburg Address,* November 19, 1863.

SEE ALSO: Civilization; Democracy 4; Equality 3; Money 3; Self-government 3; Slavery 19.

NATIONAL BANK

1. I am in favor of a national bank.—*Reputed First Political Speech*, March, 1832.

2. Our opponents say there is no express authority in the Constitution to establish a bank, and therefore, a bank is unconstitutional; but we with equal truth may say there is no express authority in the Constitution to establish a subtreasury, and, therefore, a subtreasury is unconstitutional. Who, then, has the advantage of this "express authority" argument? . . . Our position is that both are constitutional.—*Speech on Subtreasury*, December 20, 1839.

3. A national bank, properly restricted, is highly necessary and proper to the establishment and maintenance of a sound currency, and for the cheap and safe collection, keeping and disbursing of the public revenue.—*Resolution at a Whig Meeting*, March 1, 1843.

SEE ALSO: Politics 1.

NATURE

All nature—the whole world, material, moral, and intellectual—is a mine; and in Adam's day it was a wholly unexplored mine. Now, it was the destined work of Adam's race to develop, by discoveries, inventions, and improvements, the hidden treasures of this mine.—*Lecture on "Discoveries, Inventions, and Improvements,"* c. February 22, 1859.

NEGROES

1. Let it not be said I am contending for the establishment of political and social equality between the whites and blacks. I have already said the contrary. I am not combating the argument of necessity, arising from the fact that the blacks are already among us; but I am combating what is set up as moral argument for allowing them to be taken where they have never yet been—arguing against the extension of a bad thing, which, where it already exists, we must of necessity manage as we best can.—*Speech at Peoria,* October 16, 1854.

2. All I ask for the negro is that if you do not like him, let him alone. If God gave him but little, that little let him enjoy.—*Springfield Speech,* July 17, 1858.

3. I do not perceive that because the white man is to have the superior position the negro should be denied everything.—*Speech at Charleston Debate,* September 18, 1858.

4. Suppose it is true that the negro is inferior to the white in the gifts of nature; is it not the exact reverse of justice that the white should for that reason take from the negro any part of the little which he has had given him? "Give to him that is needy" is the Christian rule of charity; but "take from him that is needy" is the rule of slavery.—*Notes for Speeches,* c. October 1, 1858.

5. "In the struggle between the white man and the negro," assumes that there is a struggle, in which either the white man must enslave the negro or the

negro must enslave the white. There is no such struggle. It is merely an ingenious falsehood to degrade and brutalize the negro. Let each let the other alone, and there is no struggle about it. If it was like two wrecked seamen on a narrow plank, where each must push the other off or drown himself, I would push the negro off—or a white man either; but it is not: the plank is large enough for both. This good earth is plenty broad enough for white man and negro both, and there is no need of either pushing the other off.—*New Haven Speech,* March 6, 1860.

6. I thought that whatever negroes can be got to do as soldiers, leaves just so much less for white soldiers to do, in saving the Union. Does it appear otherwise to you? But negroes, like other people, act upon motives. Why should they do anything for us, if we will do nothing for them? If they stake their lives for us, they must be prompted by the strongest motive—even the promise of freedom. And the promise being made, must be kept.—*Letter to J. S. Conkling,* August 26, 1863.

SEE ALSO: Abolition; Emancipation; Equality 3, 6; Freedom 3; Marriage 1; Revolution 1; Self-government 3; Slavery.

– O –

OFFICE SEEKERS

1. In regard to the patronage sought with so much eagerness and jealousy, I have prescribed for myself the maxim, "Justice to all;" and I earnestly beseech your cooperation in keeping the maxim good.—*Letter to W. H. Seward,* December 8, 1860.

2. If our American society and the United States government are demoralized and overthrown, it will come from the voracious desire for office, this wriggle to live without toil, work and labor from which I am not free myself.—*Letter to W. H. Herndon,* c. 1861.

OPINION

1. Holding it a sound maxim that it is better only sometimes to be right than at all times to be wrong, so soon as I discover my opinions to be erroneous, I shall be ready to renounce them.—*Address to the People of Sangamon County,* March 9, 1832.

2. I have never tried to conceal my opinions, nor tried to deceive any one in reference to them.—*Rejoinder at Freeport Debate,* August 27, 1858.

3. If we ever have a government on the principles we profess, we should remember, while we exercise our opinion, that others have also rights to the exercise of their opinions, and that we should endeavor to allow these rights, and act in such a manner as to create no bad feeling.—*Remarks upon Sectionalism,* March 5, 1861.

SEE ALSO: Conduct 5; Error 1; Right and Wrong 1; Self-government 3.

— P —

PARTY

1. A free people in times of peace and quiet—when pressed by no common danger—naturally divide into parties. At such times the man who is of neither party is not, cannot be of any consequence.—*Eulogy on Henry Clay,* July 16, 1852.

2. The party lash and the fear of ridicule will overawe justice and liberty; for it is a singular fact, but none the less a fact, and well known by the most common experience, that men will do things under the terror of the party lash that they would not on any account or for any consideration do otherwise; while men who will march up to the mouth of a loaded cannon without shrinking, will run from the terrible name of "Abolitionist," even when pronounced by a worthless creature whom they, with good reason, despise.—*The "Lost" Speech at Bloomington,* May 29, 1856.

3. I remember being once much amused at seeing two partially intoxicated men engaged in a fight with

their greatcoats on, which fight, after a long and rather harmless contest, ended in each having fought himself out of his own coat and into that of the other. If the two leading parties of this day are really identical with the two in the days of Jefferson and Adams, they have performed the same feat.—*Letter to H. L. Pierce and Others,* April 6, 1859.

4. No party can command respect which sustains this year what it opposed last.—*Letter to S. Galloway,* July 28, 1859.

5. No party can be justly held responsible for what individual members of it may say or do.—*Letter to Governor H. R. Gamble,* October 19, 1863.

SEE ALSO: Politics 5; Self-government 3.

PAST AND PRESENT

1. Let bygones be bygones; let past differences as nothing be.—*Chicago Banquet Speech,* December 10, 1856.

2. The dogmas of the quiet past are inadequate to the stormy present. . . . As our case is new, so must we think anew and act anew.—*Annual Message to Congress,* December 1, 1862.

3. We can see the past, though we may not claim to have directed it.—*Address at Sanitary Fair,* April 18, 1864.

SEE ALSO: Quarrel 2; Selfishness 1.

PATIENCE

1. I am a patient man—always willing to forgive on the Christian terms of repentance.—*Letter to R. Johnson, July 26, 1862.*

2. A man watches his pear-tree day after day, impatient for the ripening of the fruit. Let him attempt to force the process and he may spoil both fruit and tree. But let him patiently wait, and the ripe pear at length falls into his lap.—*A Remark, c. February 3, 1865, as reported in F. B. Carpenter's Six Months at the White House, 77.*

SEE ALSO: Justice 3.

PATRIOTISM

1. He [Henry Clay] loved his country partly because it was his own country, and mostly because it was a free country; and he burned with a zeal for its advancement, prosperity, and glory, because he saw in such the advancement, prosperity, and glory of human liberty, human right, and human nature. He desired the prosperity of his countrymen, partly because they were his countrymen, but chiefly to show to the world that free men could be prosperous.—*Eulogy on Henry Clay, July 16, 1852.*

2. But let us, meanwhile, appeal to the sense and patriotism of the people, and not to their prejudice; let us spread the floods of enthusiasm here aroused all over these vast prairies so suggestive of freedom.—*The "Lost" Speech at Bloomington, May 29, 1856.*

3. In a country like this, where every man bears

on his face the marks of intelligence, where every man's clothing, if I may so speak, shows signs of comfort, and every dwelling signs of happiness and contentment, where schools and churches abound on every side, the Union can never be in danger. I would, if I could, instill some degree of patriotism and confidence into the political mind in relation to this matter.—*Remarks at Cleveland,* February 15, 1861.

4. It is gratifying to know that the expenditures made necessary by the rebellion are not beyond the resources of the loyal people, and to believe that the same patriotism which has thus far sustained the government will continue to sustain it till peace and union shall again bless the land.—*Annual Message to Congress,* December 3, 1861.

5. Gold is good in its place, but living, brave, patriotic men are better than gold.—*Response to a Serenade,* November 10, 1864.

SEE ALSO: Moderation.

PEACE

1. I shall do all that may be in my power to promote a peaceful settlement of all our difficulties. The man does not live who is more devoted to peace than I am, none who would do more to preserve it, but it may be necessary to put the foot down firmly.— *Address to the Assembly of New Jersey,* February 21, 1861.

2. Now and ever I shall do all in my power for

peace, consistently with the maintenance of the government.—*Reply to Governor Hicks and Mayor Brown*, April 20, 1861.

3. You desire peace, and you blame me that we do not have it. But how can we attain it? There are but three conceivable ways: First, to suppress the rebellion by force of arms. This I am trying to do. Are you for it? If you are, so far we are agreed. If you are not for it, a second way is to give up the Union. I am against it. Are you for it? If you are, you should say so plainly. If you are not for force nor yet for dissolution, there only remains some imaginable compromise. I do not believe any compromise embracing the maintenance of the Union is now possible. All I learn leads to a directly opposite belief.—*Letter to J. C. Conkling*, August 26, 1863.

4. To whom it may concern:

Any proposition which embraces the restoration of peace, the integrity of the whole Union, and the abandonment of slavery, and which comes by and with an authority that can control the armies now at war against the United States, will be received and considered by the executive government of the United States, and will be met by liberal terms on other substantial and collateral points, and the bearer or bearers thereof shall have safe conduct both ways.— *Announcement concerning Terms of Peace*, July 18, 1864.

5. With malice toward none, with charity for all,

with firmness in the right as God gives us to see the right, let us strive on to finish the work we are in, to bind up the nation's wounds, to care for him who shall have borne the battle and for his widow and his orphans, to do all which may achieve and cherish a just and lasting peace among ourselves and with all nations.—*Second Inaugural Address,* March 4, 1865.

SEE ALSO: Charity; Constitution 3; Party 1.

PEOPLE

1. The people know their rights, and they are never slow to assert and maintain them, when they are invaded.—*Bank Speech,* January, 1837.

2. In leaving the people's business in their own hands, we cannot be wrong.—*Speech in Congress,* July 27, 1848.

3. The people—the people—are the rightful masters of both congresses and courts—not to overthrow the Constitution, but to overthrow the men who pervert it.—*Speeches in Kansas,* December 1-5, 1859.

4. This country, with its institutions, belongs to the people who inhabit it. Whenever they shall grow weary of the existing government, they can exercise their constitutional right of amending it, or their revolutionary right to dismember or overthrow it.— *First Inaugural Address,* March 4, 1861.

5. I am, you know, only the servant of the people. —*Letter to J. R. Gilmore,* April 13, 1861.

6. The people's will, constitutionally expressed, is the ultimate law for all.—*Response to a Serenade,* October 19, 1864.

SEE ALSO: Amendments 2; Democracy 4; Equality 5; Nation 2; Supreme Court.

PERSONAL WORTH

It is difficult to make a man miserable while he feels he is worthy of himself and claims kindred to the great God who made him.—*Address on Negro Colonization,* August 14, 1862.

SEE ALSO: Ambition 1.

PERSUASION

When the conduct of men is designed to be influenced, persuasion, kind, unassuming persuasion, should be adopted. It is an old and a true maxim "that a drop of honey catches more flies than a gallon of gall." So with men. If you would win a man to your cause, first convince him that you are his sincere friend. Therein is a drop of honey that catches his heart, which, say what he will, is the great highroad to his reason, and which, when once gained, you will find but little trouble in convincing his judgment of the justice of your cause, if indeed that cause really be a just one. On the contrary, assume to dictate to man's judgment, or to command his action or to mark him out as one to be shunned and despised, and he will retreat within himself, close all the avenues to

93

his head and heart; and though your cause be naked truth itself, transformed to the heaviest lance, harder than steel and sharper than steel can be made, and though you throw it with more than herculean force and decision, you will be no more able to pierce him than to penetrate the hard shell of a tortoise with a rye straw. Such is man and so must he be understood by those who would lead him even to his own best interests.—*Temperance Address*, February 22, 1852.

PHILOSOPHY

No policy that does not rest upon philosophical public opinion can be permanently maintained.—*New Haven Speech*, March 6, 1860.

POLITICS

1. I presume you all know who I am. I am humble Abraham Lincoln. I have been solicited by many friends to become a candidate for the legislature. My politics are short and sweet, like the old woman's dance. I am in favor of a national bank. I am in favor of the internal-improvements system and a high protective tariff. These are my sentiments and political principles. If elected, I shall be thankful; if not, it will be all the same.—*Address to the People of Sangamon County*, March 9, 1832.

2. I am older in years than I am in the tricks and trades of politicians. I desire to live, and I desire place and distinction; but I would rather die now than, like the gentleman, live to see the day that I

would change my politics for an office worth $3,000 a year, and then feel compelled to erect a lightning-rod to protect a guilty conscience from an offended God.—*Speech at a Mass Meeting in Springfield, 1835.*

3. This work is exclusively the work of politicians; a set of men who have interests aside from the interests of the people, and who, to say the most of them, are, taken as a mass, at least one long step removed from honest men. I say this with greater freedom because, being a politician myself, none can regard it as personal.—*Speech before the Illinois Legislature,* January, 1837.

4. We have all heard of the animal standing in doubt between two stacks of hay and starving to death. The like of that would never happen to General Cass. Place the stacks a thousand miles apart, he would stand stock-still midway between them, and eat them both at once, and the green grass along the line would be apt to suffer some, too, at the same time. By all means make him President, gentlemen. He will feed you bounteously—if—if there is any left after he shall have helped himself.—*Speech in Congress,* July 27, 1848.

5. In this country, and in any country where freedom of thought is tolerated, citizens attach themselves to political parties. It is but an ordinary degree of charity to attribute this act to the supposition that in thus attaching themselves to the various parties, each man in his own judgment supposes he thereby best advances the interests of the whole country. And

when an election is past, it is altogether befitting a free people, as I suppose, that, until the next election, they should be one people.—*Reply to Governor Morgan of New York,* February 18, 1861.

6. It is a little singular that I, who am not a vindictive man, should have always been before the people in canvasses marked for their bitterness: always but once; when I came to Congress it was a quiet time. But always besides that the contests in which I have been prominent have been marked with great rancor.—*Letter to J. Hay,* November 8, 1864.

SEE ALSO: Moderation; Right and Wrong 8; Slavery 8.

POPULATION

By the law of increase shown in the census tables, the country may expect to number over two hundred millions of people in less than a century. And we will reach this too, if we do not ourselves relinquish the chance, by the folly and evils of disunion, or by long and exhausting war springing from the only great element of national discord among us.—*As quoted in Nicolay and Hay,* History, VI, p. 399.

SEE ALSO: Civil War 4; Equality 1; Slavery 18.

POSTERITY

1. Few can be induced to labor exclusively for posterity; and none will do it enthusiastically. Posterity has done nothing for us; and theorize on it as we may, practically we shall do very little for it, unless

we are made to think we are at the same time doing something for ourselves.—*Temperance Addresss*, February 22, 1842.

2. May our children and our children's children for a thousand generations continue to enjoy the benefits conferred upon us by a united country and have cause yet to rejoice under those glorious institutions bequeathed us by Washington and his compeers!—*Remarks at Frederick*, October 4, 1862.

SEE ALSO: Liberty 3.

POVERTY

1. I am not ashamed to confess that twenty-five years ago I was a hired laborer, mauling rails, at work on a flatboat—just what might happen to any poor man's son. I want every man to have a chance.—*Speech at New Haven*, March 6, 1860.

2. No men are more worthy to be trusted than those who toil up from poverty—none less inclined to take or touch aught which they have not honestly earned.—*Annual Message to Congress*, December 3, 1861.

SEE ALSO: Land 2.

PRAISE

Let us be sure that, in giving praise to certain individuals, we do no injustice to others.—*Reply to Serenade*, September 24, 1862.

PRAYER

Neither party expected for the war the magnitude or the duration which it has already attained. . . . Both read the same Bible, and pray to the same God; and each invokes His aid against the other. It may seem strange that any men should dare to ask a just God's assistance in wringing their bread from the sweat of other men's faces; but let us judge not, that we be not judged. The prayers of both could not be answered—that of neither has been answered fully. The Almighty has his own purposes.—*Second Inaugural Address,* March 4, 1865.

SEE ALSO: War 5.

PRESIDENCY

1. The Presidency, even to the most experienced politicians, is no bed of roses.—*Speech at Chicago,* July 25, 1850.

2. In my present position it is hardly proper for me to make speeches. Every word is so closely noted that it will not do to make foolish ones, and I cannot be expected to be prepared to make sensible ones. If I were as I have been most of my life, I might, perhaps, talk nonsense to you for half an hour, and it wouldn't hurt anybody.—*Speech at Frederick,* October 4, 1862.

SEE ALSO: Liberty 7; Silence.

PRINCIPLES

1. We are here to stand firmly for a principle—to stand firmly for a right. We know that great political and moral wrongs are done, and outrages committed, and we denounce those wrongs and outrages, although we cannot, at present, do much more. But we desire to reach out beyond those personal outrages and establish a rule that will apply to all, and so prevent any future outrages.—*The "Lost" Speech at Bloomington,* May 29, 1856.

2. Compromises of principle break down of their own weight.—*Letter to J. J. Crittenden,* December 22, 1859.

3. Important principles may and must be inflexible.—*Last Public Address,* April 11, 1865.

SEE ALSO: Politics 1.

PRINTING

But to return to the consideration of printing, it is plain that it is but the other half, and in reality the better half, of writing; and that both together are but the assistants of speech in the communication of thoughts between man and man. When man was possessed of speech alone, the chances of invention, discovery, and improvement were very limited; but by the introduction of each of these they were greatly multiplied. When writing was invented, any important observation likely to lead to a discovery had at least a chance of being written down, and consequently a little chance of never being forgotten, and of being seen and reflected upon by a much greater number of persons; and thereby the chances of a valuable hint being caught proportionately augmented. By this means the observation of a single individual might lead to an important invention years, and even centuries, after he was dead. In one word, by means of writing, the seeds of invention were more permanently preserved and more widely sown. And yet for three thousand years, during which printing remained undiscovered after writing was in use, it was only a small portion of the people who could write, or read writing; and consequently the field of invention, though much extended, still continued very limited. At length printing came. It gave ten thousand copies of any written matter quite as cheaply as ten were given before; and consequently a thousand minds were brought into the field where there was but one before. This was a great gain—and history shows a great change corresponding to it—in point of time. I will venture to consider it the true termination of that period called "the dark ages."—*Lecture before the Springfield Library Association,* February 22, 1860.

PROGRESS

1. Advancement—improvement in condition—is the order of things in a society of equals.—*A Fragment on Slavery,* c. July 1, 1854.

2. I do not mean to say we are bound to follow implicitly in whatever our fathers did. To do so would be to discard all the lights of current experi-

ence—to reject all progress, all improvement. What I do say is if we would supplant the opinions and policy of our fathers in any case, we should do so upon evidence so conclusive, and argument so clear, that even their great authority, fairly considered and weighed, cannot stand.—*Address at Cooper Institute*, February 27, 1860.

3. I hold that while man exists it is his duty to improve not only his own condition, but to assist in ameliorating mankind; and therefore, I will simply say that I am for those means which will give the greatest good to the greatest number.—*Address to Germans in Cincinnati*, February 12, 1861.

SEE ALSO: Labor 6.

PROMISE

1. We must not promise what we ought not, lest we be called on to perform what we cannot.—*The "Lost" Speech at Bloomington*, May 29, 1856.

2. Bad promises are better broken than kept.—*Last Public Speech*, April 11, 1865.

SEE ALSO: Conduct 2; Hope 2; Negroes 6.

PROPERTY

1. The love of property and a consciousness of right or wrong have conflicting places in our organization, which often make a man's course seem crooked, his conduct a riddle.—*Hartford Speech*, March 5, 1860.

2. The slave-holder does not like to be considered a mean fellow for holding that species of property,

and hence he has to struggle within himself, and sets about arguing himself into the belief that slavery is right. The property influences his mind. The dissenting minister who argued some theological point with one of the Established Church was always met by the reply, "I can't see it so." He opened the Bible and pointed him to a passage, but the orthodox minister replied, "I can't see it so." Then he showed him a single word—"Can you see that?" "Yes, I see it," was the reply. The dissenter laid a guinea over the word, and asked, "Do you see it now?" So here. Whether the owners of this species of property do really see it as it is, it is not for me to say; but if they do, they see it as it is through two billions of dollars, and that is a pretty thick coating. Certain it is that they do not see it as we see it. Certain it is that this two thousand million of dollars invested in this species of property is all so concentrated that the mind can grasp it at once. This immense pecuniary interest has its influence upon their minds.—*New Haven Speech,* March 6, 1860.

3. Property is the fruit of labor; property is desirable; is a positive good in the world. That some should be rich shows that others may become rich, and hence is just encouragement to industry and enterprise. Let not him who is houseless pull down the house of another, but let him work diligently and build one for himself, thus by example assuring that his own shall be safe from violence when built.— *Reply to New York Workingmen,* March 21, 1864.

SEE ALSO: Army 2; Democracy 3; Public Opinion 6; Slavery 15, 16, 18; Taxes; War 4; Wealth 1.

PROSPERITY

1. What is it that we hold most dear among us? Our own liberty and prosperity.—*Reply at Alton Debate,* October 15, 1858.

2. By the best cultivation of the physical world beneath and around us, and the intellectual and moral world within us, we shall secure an individual, social, and political prosperity and happiness, whose course shall be onward and upward, and which, while the earth endures, shall not pass away.—*Address before the Wisconsin State Agricultural Society,* September 30, 1859.

SEE ALSO: Liberty 3; Patriotism 1.

PROVIDENCE

1. I believe in the providence of the most men, the largest purse, and the longest cannon.—*Speech at Springfield,* 1856.

2. I hope it will not be irreverent for me to say that if it is probable that God would reveal his will to others on a point so connected with my duty, it might be supposed He would reveal it directly to me; for, unless I am more deceived in myself than I often am, it is my earnest desire to know the will of Providence in this matter. And if I can learn what it is, I will do it.

These are not, however, the days of miracles, and

I suppose it will be granted that I am not to expect a direct revelation. I must study the plain physical facts of the case, ascertain what is possible, and learn what appears to be wise and right.—*Reply to a Committee from Religious Denominations of Chicago,* September 13, 1862.

SEE ALSO: Immigrants 3.

PUBLIC OPINION

1. There is both a power and a magic in popular opinion.—*The "Lost" Speech at Bloomington,* May 29, 1856.

2. Our government rests in public opinion. Whoever can change public opinion can change the government practically just so much.—*Chicago Banquet Speech,* December 10, 1856.

3. In this age, and in this country, public sentiment is everything. With it, nothing can fail; against it, nothing can succeed. Whoever molds public sentiment goes deeper than he who enacts statutes or pronounces judicial decisions. He makes possible the enforcement of them, else impossible.—*Notes for Speeches,* c. October 1, 1858.

4. We know that in a government like this, a government of the people, where the voice of all the men of the country, substantially, enters into the administration of the government, what lies at the bottom of all of it is public opinion.—*Speech at Cincinnati,* September 17, 1859.

5. Public opinion settles everything here. Any

policy to be permanent must have public opinion at the bottom—something in accordance with the human mind as it is.—*Hartford Speech*, March 5, 1860.

6. Public opinion is founded, to a great extent, on a property basis.—*Hartford Speech*, March 5, 1860.

SEE ALSO: Liquor; Slavery 18.

PUNCTUATION

With educated people, I suppose, punctuation is a matter of rule; with me it is a matter of feeling. But I must say I have great respect for the semicolon; it's a useful little chap.—*Letter to N. Brooks*, December 3, 1864.

PUNISHMENT

How effectual have penitentiaries heretofore been in preventing the crimes they were established to suppress? Has not confinement in them long been the legal penalty of larceny, forgery, robbery, and many other crimes, in almost all the States? And yet are not those crimes committed weekly, daily—nay, and even hourly—in every one of those States? Again, the gallows has long been the penalty of murder, and yet we scarcely open a newspaper that does not relate a new case of that crime. If, then, the penitentiary has ever heretofore failed to prevent larceny, forgery, and robbery, and the gallows and halter have likewise failed to prevent murder, by what process of reasoning, I ask, is it that we are to conclude the penitentiary will hereafter prevent the stealing of the public money? But our opponents seem to think they answer that charge that the money will be stolen fully if they can show that they will bring the offenders to punishment. Not so. Will the punishment of the thief bring back the stolen money? No more so than the hanging of a murderer restores his victim to life. What is the object desired? Certainly not the greatest number of thieves we can catch, but that the money may not be stolen.—*Speech on Subtreasury*, December 20, 1839.

SEE ALSO: Civilization; Mob Law 1.

PURPOSE

Men are not flattered by being shown that there has been a difference of purpose between the Almighty and them.—*Letter to T. Weed*, March 15, 1865.

SEE ALSO: Purpose.

– Q –

QUARREL

1. Quarrel not at all. No man resolved to make the most of himself can spare time for personal contention. Still less can he afford to take all the consequences, including the vitiating of his temper and the loss of self-control. Yield larger things to which you can show no more than equal right; and yield lesser ones, though clearly your own. Better give your path to a dog than be bitten by him in contesting for the right.—*Letter to J. M. Cutts,* October 26, 1863.

2. A man has not time to spend half his life in quarrels. If a man ceases to attack me, I never remember the past against him.—*A Remark to People in Stanton's Office,* November 8, 1864.

– R –

READING

A capacity and taste for reading gives access to whatever has already been discovered by others. It is the key, or one of the keys, to the already solved problems. And not only so; it gives a relish and facility for successfully pursuing the unsolved ones.—*Address before the Wisconsin State Agricultural Society*, September 30, 1859.

SEE ALSO: Books; Education 1; Printing.

REASON

1. Passion has helped us; but can do so no more. It will in future be our enemy. Reason, cold, calculating, unimpassioned reason, must furnish all the materials for our future support and defence. Let those materials be moulded into general intelligence, sound morality, and, in particular, a reverence for the Constitution and laws.—*Lyceum Address*, January 27, 1837.

2. Happy day when—all appetites controlled, all

poisons subdued, all matter subjected—mind, all-conquering mind, shall live and move, the monarch of the world. Glorious consummation! Hail, fall of fury! Reign of reason, all hail.—*Temperance Address,* February 22, 1842.

3. There are two ways of establishing a proposition. One is by trying to demonstrate it upon reason, and the other is to show that great men in former times have thought so and so, and thus to pass it by the weight of pure authority.—*Speech at Columbus,* September 16, 1859.

SEE ALSO: History 1.

REGRETS

Broken eggs cannot be mended; but Louisiana has nothing to do now but take her place in the Union as it was, barring the already broken eggs.— *Letter to A. Belmont,* July 31, 1862.

SEE ALSO: Amnesty 2.

RELIGION

1. I know there is a God, and that He hates injustice and slavery. I see the storm coming, and I know His hand is in it. If He has a place and work for me, and I think He has, I believe I am ready. I am nothing, but truth is everything. I know I am right, for Christ teaches it, and Christ is God.—*Letter to N. Bateman,* c. 1860.

2. I have never united myself to any church, be· cause I have found difficulty in giving my assent,

without mental reservation, to the long, complicated statements of Christian doctrine which characterize their Articles of Belief and Confessions of Faith. When any church will inscribe over its altar, as its sole qualification for membership, the Saviour's condensed statement of the substance of both Law and Gospel, "Thou shalt love the Lord thy God with all thy heart, and with all thy soul, and with all thy mind, and thy neighbor, as thyself," that church will I join with all my heart and all my soul.—*A Remark to H. C. Demig, c. 1862.*

3. I have never interfered nor thought of interfering as to who shall or who shall not preach in any church; nor have I knowingly or believingly tolerated any one else to so interfere by my authority. If any one is so interfering by color of my authority, I would like to have it specifically made known to me. . . . I will not have control of any church on any side.—*Letter to O. D. Filley,* December 22, 1863.

4. The religion that sets men to rebel and fight against their government, because, as they think, that government does not sufficiently help some men to eat their bread in the sweat of other men's faces, is not the sort of religion upon which people can get to heaven.—*A Remark,* December 3, 1864.

SEE ALSO: Education 1; Right and Wrong 8.

RESPONSIBILITY

1. It strikes me there is some difference between holding a man responsible for an act which he has

not done, and holding him responsible for an act that he has done.—*Rejoinder at Quincy Debate,* October 13, 1858.

2. In times like the present, men should utter nothing for which they would not willingly be responsible through time and eternity.—*Annual Message to Congress,* December 1, 1862.

SEE ALSO: Party 5.

REVOLUTION

1. I read once, in a blackletter law book, "a slave is a human being who is legally not a *person* but a *thing*." And if the safeguards to liberty are broken down, as is now attempted, when they have made things of all the free negroes, how long, think you, before they begin to make things of poor white men? Be not deceived. Revolutions do not go backward. The founder of the Democratic party declared that *all* men were created equal. His successor in the leadership has written the word "white" before men, making it read "all white men are created equal." Pray, will or may not the Know-nothings, if they should get in power, add the word "Protestant," making it read "all Protestant white men"?—*The "Lost" Speech at Bloomington,* May 29, 1856.

2. If by the mere force of numbers a majority should deprive a minority of any clearly written constitutional right, it might, in a moral point of view, justify revolution—certainly would if such a right were a vital one.—*First Inaugural Address,* March 4, 1861.

111

3. Any people anywhere being inclined and having the power have the right to rise up and shake off the existing government, and form a new one that suits them better. This is a most valuable, a most sacred right—a right which we hope and believe is to liberate the world. Nor is this right confined to cases in which the whole people of an existing government may choose to exercise it. Any portion of such people that can may revolutionize and make their own of so much of the territory as they inhabit. More than this, a majority of any portion of such people may revolutionize, putting down a minority, intermingled with or near about them, who may oppose this movement. Such a minority was precisely the case of the Tories of our own revolution. It is a quality of revolutions not to go by old ideas or old laws; but to break up both, and make new ones.—*Mexican War Speech,* January 12, 1848.

SEE ALSO: Majority 3; People 4; States 2.

RIGHT AND WRONG
1. Holding it a sound maxim that it is better only sometimes to be right than at all times wrong, so soon as I discover my opinions to be erroneous I shall be ready to renounce them.—*Address to the People of Sangamon County,* March 9, 1832.

2. You must remember that some things legally right are not morally right.—*A Letter to W. H. Herndon,* 1848.

112

3. Stand with anybody that stands right. Stand with him while he is right, and part with him when he goes wrong.—*Speech at Peoria*, October 16, 1854.

4. Do they really think that by right surrendering to wrong the hopes of our Constitution, our Union, and our liberties can possibly be bettered?—*Fragment on Sectionalism*, October 1, 1856.

5. You cannot institute any equality between right and wrong.—*Reply at Galesburg Debate*, October 7, 1858.

6. It is the eternal struggle between these two principles—right and wrong—throughout the world. They are two principles that have stood face to face from the beginning of time; and will ever continue to struggle. The one is the common right of humanity, and the other the divine right of kings. It is the same principle in whatever shape it develops itself. It is the same spirit that says, "You toil and work and earn bread, and I'll eat it." No matter in what shape it comes, whether from the mouth of a king who seeks to bestride the people of his own nation and live by the fruit of their labor, or from one race of men as an apology for enslaving another race, it is the same tyrannical principle.—*Reply at Alton Debate*, October 15, 1858.

7. Let us have the faith that right makes might; and in that faith let us to the end dare to do our duty as we understand it.—*Address at Cooper Institute*, February 27, 1860.

8. You say that you think slavery a wrong, but you renounce all attempts to restrain it. Is there anything else that you think wrong, that you are not willing to deal with as a wrong? Why are you so careful, so tender of this one wrong and no other? You will not let us do a single thing as if it was wrong; there is no place where you will allow it to be even called wrong. We must not call it wrong in the free States, because it is not there; we must not call it wrong in the slave States, because it is there; we must not call it wrong in politics, because that is bringing morality into politics, and we must not call it wrong in the pulpit, because that is bringing politics into religion; we must not bring it into the tract society, or other societies, because those are such unsuitable places, and there is no single place, according to you, where this wrong thing can properly be called wrong.—*New Haven Speech,* March 6, 1860.

9. At all events, I must keep some consciousness of being somewhere near right.—*A Remark,* July 4, 1864.

SEE ALSO: Bible; God 4; Mob Law 2; Opinion 1; Property 1; Slavery 19.

RIGHTS

I believe each individual is naturally entitled to do as he pleases with himself and the fruit of his labor, so far as it in no wise interferes with any other man's rights; that each community, as a state, has a

114

right to do exactly as it pleases with all the concerns within that State that interfere with the right of no other State; and that the general government, upon principle, has no right to interfere with anything other than that general class of things that does not concern the whole.—*Chicago Speech,* July 10, 1858.

SEE ALSO: Capital; Despotism 3; Majority 3; Opinion 3; Peace 1.

SELF-GOVERNMENT

1. According to our ancient faith, the just powers of governments are derived from the consent of the governed. Now the relation of master and slave is *pro tanto* a total violation of this principle. The master not only governs the slave without his consent, but he governs him by a set of rules altogether different from those which he prescribes for himself. Allow all the governed an equal voice in the government, and that, and that only, is self-government.—*Speech at Peoria,* October 16, 1854.

2. I have said very many times . . . that no man believed more than I in the principle of self-government; that it lies at the bottom of all my ideas of just government from beginning to end.—*Chicago Speech,* July 10, 1858.

3. Judge Douglas is a man of large influence. His bare opinion goes far to fix the opinions of others. Besides this, thousands hang their hopes upon forcing their opinions to agree with his. It is a party neces-

sity with them to say they agree with him, and there is danger they will repeat the saying till they really come to believe it. Others dread, and shrink from, his denunciations, his sarcasms, and his ingenious misrepresentations. The susceptible young hear lessons from him, such as their fathers never heard when they were young. If, by all these means, he shall succeed in molding public sentiment to a perfect accordance with his own; in bringing all men to endorse all court decisions, without caring to know whether they are right or wrong; in bringing all tongues to as perfect a silence as his own, as to there being any wrong in slavery; in bringing all to declare, with him, that care not whether slavery be voted down or voted up; that if any people want slaves they have a right to have them; that negroes are not men; have no part in the Declaration of Independence; that there is no moral question about slavery; that liberty and slavery are perfectly consistent—indeed, necessary accompaniments; that for a strong man to declare himself the superior of a weak one, and thereupon enslave the weak one, is the very essence of liberty, the most sacred right of self-government; when, I say, public sentiment shall be brought to all this, in the name of Heaven what barrier will be left against slavery being made lawful everywhere?—*Notes for Speeches,* c. October 1, 1858.

4. Well, I, too, believe in self-government as I understand it; but I do not understand that the privilege one man takes of making a slave of another,

or holding him as such, is any part of "self-govern-ment." To call it so is, to my mind, simply absurd and ridiculous. I am for the people of the whole nation doing just as they please in all matters which concern the whole nation; for those of each part do-ing just as they choose in all matters which concern no other part; and for each individual doing just as he chooses in all matters which concern nobody else. This is the principle.—*Notes for Speeches,* c. October 1, 1858.

SEE ALSO: Despotism 1; Government 1; Slavery 7; Sovereignty.

SELFISHNESS

1. All mankind in the past, present and future in all their actions are moved and controlled by a mo-tive, and, at bottom, the snaky tongue of selfishness will wag out.—c. 1860, *as quoted in the Abraham Lin-coln Quarterly for December,* 1941.

2. We have been mistaken all our lives if we do not know that whites, as well as blacks, look to their self-interest.—*Address on Negro Colonization,* August 14, 1862.

SEE ALSO: Slavery 6.

SILENCE

I have not kept silence since the presidential elec-tion from any party wantonness, or from any indiffer-ence to the anxiety that pervades the minds of men about the aspect of the political affairs of the country. I have kept silence for the reason that I supposed it was peculiarly proper that I should do so until the time came when, according to the custom of the country, I could speak officially.—*Address at New York City,* February 19, 1861.

SEE ALSO: Meaning.

SKILL

Every man is proud of what he does well, and no man is proud of what he does not do well. With the former, his heart is in his work; and he will do twice as much of it with less fatigue; the latter he performs a little imperfectly, looks at it in disgust, turns from it, and imagines himself exceedingly tired. The little he has done comes to nothing for want of finishing.—*Address before the Wisconsin State Agricultural Society,* September 30, 1859.

SEE ALSO: Leadership 2.

SLANDER

If you think you can slander a woman into loving you or a man into voting for you, try it till you are satisfied.—*New Haven Speech,* March 6, 1860.

SLAVERY

1. The ant who has toiled and dragged a crumb to his nest will furiously defend the fruit of his labor against whatever robber assails him. So plain that the most dumb and stupid slave that ever toiled for a master does constantly know that he is wronged. So

plain that no one, high or low, ever does mistake it, except in a plainly selfish way; for although volume upon volume is written to prove slavery a very good thing, we never hear of the man who wishes to take the good of it by being a slave himself.—*A Fragment on Slavery,* c. July 1, 1854.

2. If A can prove, however conclusively, that he may of right enslave B, why may not B snatch the same argument and prove equally that he may enslave A? You say A is white and B is black. It is color, then; the lighter having the right to enslave the darker? Take care. By this rule you are to be slave to the first man you meet with a fairer skin than your own. You do not mean color exactly? You mean the whites are intellectually the superiors of the blacks, and therefore have the right to enslave them? Take care again. By this rule you are to be slave to the first man you meet with an intellect superior to your own. But, say you, it is a question of interest, and if you make it your interest you have the right to enslave another. Very well. And if he can make it his interest he has the right to enslave you.—*A Fragment on Slavery,* c. July 1, 1854.

3. This declared indifference, but, as I must think, covert real zeal, for the spread of slavery, I cannot but hate. I hate it because of the monstrous injustice of slavery itself. I hate it because it deprives our republican example of its just influence in the world; enables the enemies of free institutions with plausibility to taunt us as hypocrites; causes the real friends of free-

dom to doubt our sincerity; and especially because it forces so many good men among ourselves into an open war with the very fundamental principles of civil liberty, criticizing the Declaration of Independence, and insisting that there is no right principle of action but self-interest.—*Speech at Peoria,* October 16, 1854.

4. I have no prejudice against the Southern people. They are just what we would be in their situation. If slavery did not now exist among them, they would not introduce it. If it did now exist among us, we should not instantly give it up. This I believe of the masses North and South. Doubtless there are individuals on both sides who would not hold slaves under any circumstances, and others who would gladly introduce slavery anew if it were out of existence.—*Speech at Peoria,* October 16, 1854.

5. Whatever slavery is it has been first introduced without law.—*Speech at Peoria,* October 16, 1854.

6. Slavery is founded in the selfishness of man's nature—opposition to it in his love of justice.—*Speech at Peoria,* October 16, 1854.

7. Little by little, but steadily as man's march to the grave, we have been giving up the old for the new faith. Near eighty years ago we began by declaring that all men are created equal; but now from that beginning we have run down to the other declaration, that for some men to enslave others is a "sacred right of self-government." These principles cannot stand together. They are as opposite as God and

Mammon; and whoever holds to the one must despise the other.—*Speech at Peoria,* October 16, 1854.

8. The slave breeders and slave traders are a small, odious, and detested class among you; and yet in politics they dictate the course of all of you, and are as completely your masters as you are the masters of your negroes.—*Letter to J. F. Speed,* August 24, 1855.

9. However much you may argue upon it, or smother in soft phrase, slavery can be maintained only by force—by violence.—*The "Lost" Speech at Bloomington,* May 29, 1856.

10. It is a very strange thing, and not solvable by any moral law that I know of, that if a man loses his horse, the whole country will turn to help hang the thief but if a man but a shade or two darker than I am is himself stolen, the very crowd will hang one who aids in restoring him to liberty. Such are the inconsistencies of slavery, where a horse is more sacred than a man.—*The "Lost" Speech at Bloomington,* May 29, 1856.

11. If we cannot give freedom to every creature, let us do nothing that will impose slavery upon any other creature.—*Chicago Speech,* July 10, 1858.

12. Suppose it is true that the negro is inferior to the white in the gifts of nature; is it not the exact reverse of justice that the white should for that reason take from the negro any part of the little which he has had given him? "Give to him that is needy" is the Christian rule of charity; but "Take from him that is

needy" is the rule of slavery.—*Notes for Speeches, c.* October 1, 1858.

13. When the fathers of the government cut off the source of slavery by the abolition of the slave-trade, and adopted a system of restricting it from the new Territories where it had not existed, I maintain that they placed it where they understood, and all sensible men understood, it was in the course of ultimate extinction.—*Rejoinder at Quincy Debate,* October 13, 1858.

14. There is no justification for prohibiting slavery anywhere, save only in the assumption that slavery is wrong.—*Speeches in Kansas,* December 1-5, 1859.

15. Slaves are property, and only property.—*Speech at Leavenworth,* December 3, 1859.

16. Neither the word "slave" nor "slavery" is to be found in the Constitution, nor the word "property" even, in any connection with language alluding to the things slave or slavery.—*Address at Cooper Institute,* February 27, 1860.

17. If slavery is right, it ought to be extended; if not, it ought to be restricted—there is no middle ground.—*Hartford Speech,* March 5, 1860.

18. One sixth, and a little more, of the population of the United States are slaves, looked upon as property, as nothing but property. The cash value of these slaves, at a moderate estimate, is $2,000,000,000. This amount of property value has a vast influence on the minds of its owners, very naturally. The same amount of property would have an equal influence upon us

if owned in the North. . . . Public opinion is founded, to a great extent, on a property basis. What lessens the value of property is opposed; what enhances its value is favored. Public opinion at the South regards slaves as property, and insists upon treating them like other property.—*Hartford Speech,* March 5, 1860.

19. If slavery is right, all words, acts, laws, and constitutions against it are themselves wrong, and should be silenced and swept away. If it is right, we cannot justly object to its nationality—its universality; if it is wrong, they cannot justly insist upon its extension—its enlargement. All they ask we could readily grant, if we thought slavery right; all we ask they could as readily grant, if they thought it wrong. Their thinking it right, and our thinking it wrong, is the precise fact upon which depends the whole controversy. Thinking it right, as they do, they are not to blame for desiring its full recognition as being right; but thinking it wrong, as we do, can we yield to them? Can we cast our votes with their view, and against our own? In view of our moral, social, and political responsibilities, can we do this? Wrong as we think slavery is, we can yet afford to let it alone where it is, because that much is due to the necessity arising from its actual presence in the nation.—*New Haven Speech,* March 6, 1860.

20. I am naturally anti-slavery. If slavery is not wrong, nothing is wrong. I cannot remember when I did not so think and feel.—*Letter to A. G. Hodges,* April 4, 1864.

21. I have always thought that all men should be free; but if any should be slaves, it should be first those who desire it for themselves, and secondly, those who desire it for others. When I hear anyone arguing for slavery, I feel a strong impulse to see it tried on him personally.—*Address to Indiana Regiment,* March 17, 1865.

SEE ALSO: Abolition; Civil War 3, 5; Declaration of Independence 1; Despotism 2; Emancipation; Freedom 3, 4; Government 5; Negroes; Peace 4; Property 2; Self-government 1, 4; Union 3.

SMALL THINGS

The smallest are often the most difficult things to deal with.—*Reply at Jonesboro Debate,* September 15, 1858.

SOLDIERS

This extraordinary war in which we are engaged falls heavily upon all classes of people, but the most heavily upon the soldier. For it has been said, all that a man hath will he give for his life; and while all contribute of their substance, the soldier puts his life at stake, and often yields it up in his country's cause. The highest merit, then, is due to the soldier.—*Address at Sanitary Fair,* March 16, 1864.

SEE ALSO: Army; Liquor; Mining 3; Negroes 6.

SOVEREIGNTY

1. Popular sovereignty . . . means the sovereignty of the people over their own affairs—in other words, the right of the people to govern themselves.—*Speech at Paris, Ill.,* September 8, 1858.

2. I think a definition of genuine popular sovereignty, in the abstract, would be about this: That each man shall do precisely as he pleases with himself, and with all those things that exclusively concern him. Applied to government, this principle would be that a general government shall do all those things which pertain to it, and all the local governments shall do precisely as they please in respect to those matters which exclusively concern them. I understand that this government of the United States, under which we live, is based upon this principle.—*Speech at Columbus,* September 16, 1859.

3. There is a broad distinction between real popular sovereignty and Douglas popular sovereignty. That the nation shall control what concerns it; that a State, or any minor political community, shall control what exclusively concerns it; and that an individual shall control what exclusively concerns him—is a real popular sovereignty . . . Douglas popular sovereignty, as a matter of principle, simply is: "If one man would enslave another, neither that other nor any third man has a right to object."—*Speeches in Kansas,* December 1-5, 1859.

4. What is "sovereignty" in the popular sense of the term? Would it be far wrong to define it "a

political community without a political superior?"—
Message to Congress, July 4, 1861.

SEE ALSO: Majority 2; Squatter Sovereignty; States 3.

SPEECH

The inclination to exchange thoughts with one another is probably an original impulse of our nature. If I be in pain, I wish to let you know it, and to ask your sympathy and assistance; and my pleasurable emotions I also wish to communicate to and share with you. But to carry on such communications, some instrumentality is indispensable. Accordingly, speech —articulate sounds rattled off from the tongue—was used by our first parents, and even by Adam before the creation of Eve. He gave names to the animals while she was still a bone in his side; and he broke out quite volubly when she first stood before him, the best present of his Maker. From this it would appear that speech was not an invention of man, but rather the direct gift of his Creator. But whether divine gift or invention, it is still plain that if a mode of communication had been left to invention, speech must have been the first, from the superior adaptation to the end of the organs of speech over every other means within the whole range of nature. Of the organs of speech the tongue is the principal and if we shall test it, we shall find the capacities of the tongue, in the utterance of articulate sounds, absolutely wonderful. You can count from one to one hundred quite distinctly in about forty seconds. In doing this two hundred and eighty-three distinct sounds or syllables are uttered, being seven to each second, and yet there should be enough difference between every two to be easily recognized by the ear of the hearer. What other signs to represent things could possibly be produced so rapidly, or, even if ready made, could be arranged so rapidly to express the sense? Motions with the hands are no adequate substitute. Marks for the recognition of the eye—writing —although a wonderful auxiliary of speech, is no worthy substitute for it. In addition to the more slow and laborious process of getting up a communication in writing, the materials—pen, ink, and paper—are not always at hand. But one always has his tongue with him, and the breath of his life is the every-ready material with which it works. Speech, then, by enabling different individuals to interchange thought, and thereby to combine their powers of observation and reflection, greatly facilitates useful discoveries and inventions. What one observes, and would himself infer nothing from, he tells to another, and that other at once sees a valuable hint in it. A result is thus reached which neither alone would have arrived at.— *Speech before the Springfield Library Association,* February 22, 1859.

SEE ALSO: Printing.

SQUATTER SOVEREIGNTY

What was squatter sovereignty? I suppose if it had any significance at all, it was the right of people to govern themselves, to be sovereign in their own affairs while they were squatted down on a Territory that did not belong to them, in the sense that a State belongs to the people who inhabit it—when it belonged to the nation—such right to govern themselves was called "squatter sovereignty."—*Chicago Speech,* July 10, 1858.

SEE ALSO: Sovereignty.

STATES

1. The maintenance inviolate of the rights of the states, and especially the right of each state to order and control its own domestic institutions according to its own judgment exclusively, is essential to that balance of powers on which the perfection of our political fabric depends; and I denounce the lawless invasion by armed force of the soil of any state or territory, no matter under what pretext, as the gravest of crimes.—*Letter to D. Green,* December 28, 1860.

2. The States have their status in the Union, and they have no other legal status. If they break from this they can only do so against law and by revolution.—*Message to Congress,* July 4, 1861.

3. Much is said about the "sovereignty" of the States; but the word even is not in the National Constitution, nor, as is believed, in any of the State constitutions.—*Message to Congress,* July 4, 1861.

SEE ALSO: Government 5; Punishment; Rights.

SUCCESS

1. Let none falter, who thinks he is right, and we may succeed.—*Speech at Springfield,* December 26, 1839.

2. Always bear in mind that your own resolution to succeed is more important than any other one thing.—*Letter to I. Reaves,* November 5, 1855.

3. Success does not so much depend on external help as on self-reliance.—*Address on Negro Colonization,* August 14, 1862.

4. I say "try;" if we never try, we shall never succeed.—*Letter to General G. B. McClellan,* October 13, 1862.

5. We can succeed only by concert. It is not "Can any of us imagine better?" but, "Can we all do better?"—*Annual Message to Congress,* December 1, 1862.

SEE ALSO: Public Opinion 3.

SUPREME COURT

If the policy of the government, upon vital questions affecting the whole people, is to be irrevocably fixed by decisions of the Supreme Court . . . the people will have ceased to be their own rulers, having to that extent practically resigned their government into the hands of that eminent tribunal.—*First Inaugural Address,* March 4, 1861.

SUSPICION

I believe we need nothing so much as to get rid of unjust suspicions of one another.—*Letter to C. L. Wilson,* June 1, 1858.

– T –

TARIFF

The tariff question must be as durable as the government itself. It is a question of national housekeeping. It is to the government what replenishing the meal-tub is to the family. Ever-varying circumstances will require frequent modifications as to the amount needed and the sources of supply. So far there is little difference of opinion among the people. It is as to whether, and how far, duties on imports shall be adjusted to favor home production in the home market, that controversy begins. One party insists that such adjustment oppresses one class for the advantage of another; while the other party argues that, with all its incidents, in the long run all classes are benefited. . . . We should do neither more nor less than we gave the people reason to believe we would when they gave us their votes. . . . I have long thought it would be to our advantage to produce any necessary article at home which can be made of as good quality and with as little labor at home as abroad, at least by the difference of the carrying from abroad. In such case the carrying is demonstrably a dead loss of labor. For instance, labor being the true standard of value, is it not plain that if equal labor get a bar of railroad iron out of a mine in England, and another out of a mine in Pennsylvania, each can be laid down in a track at home cheaper than they could exchange countries, at least by the carriage? If there be a present cause why one can be both made and carried cheaper in money price than the other can be made without carrying, that cause is an unnatural and injurious one, and ought gradually, if not rapidly, to be removed.—*Address at Pittsburgh,* February 15, 1861.

SEE ALSO: Politics 1.

TAXES

It is fair that each man pay taxes in exact proportion to the value of his property, but if we should wait before collecting a tax, to adjust the taxes upon each man in exact proportion with every other man, we should never collect any tax at all.—*Address to 164th Ohio Regiment,* August 18, 1864.

SEE ALSO: Civil War 6; War 4.

TEACHING

That the committee on education be instructed to inquire into the expediency of providing by law for the examination as to the qualifications of persons offering themselves as school teachers, that no teacher shall receive any part of the public school fund who shall not have successfully passed such examination. —*Resolution in the Illinois Legislature,* December 2, 1840.

SEE ALSO: Education.

TEMPERANCE

1. Although the temperance cause has been in progress for near twenty years, it is apparent to all that it is just now being crowned with a degree of success hitherto unparalleled.

The list of its friends is daily swelled by the additions of fifties, of hundreds, and of thousands. The cause itself seems suddenly tranformed from a cold abstract theory to a living, breathing, active, and powerful chieftain, going forth "conquering and to conquer." The citadels of his great adversary are daily being stormed and dismantled; his temple and his altars, where the rites of his idolatrous worship have long been performed, and where human sacrifices have long been wont to be made, are daily desecrated and deserted. The triumph of the conqueror's fame is sounding from hill to hill, from sea to sea, and from land to land, and calling millions to his standard at a blast.

For this new and splendid success we heartily rejoice. . . . The warfare heretofore waged against the demon intemperance has somehow or other been erroneous. Either the champions engaged or the tactics they adopted have not been the most proper. These champions for the most part have been preachers, lawyers, and hired agents. Between these and the mass of mankind there is a want of approachability, if the term be admissible, partially, at least, fatal to their success. They are supposed to have no sympathy of feeling or interest with those very persons whom it is their object to convince and persuade.

And again, it is so common and so easy to ascribe motives to men of these classes other than those they profess to act upon. The preacher, it is said, advocates temperance because he is a fanatic, and desires a union of the church and state; the lawyer from his pride and vanity of hearing himself speak; and the hired agent for his salary. But when one who has long been known as a victim of intemperance bursts the fetters that have bound him, and appears before his neighbors "clothed and in his right mind," a redeemed specimen of long-lost humanity, and stands up, with tears of joy trembling in his eyes, to tell of the miseries once endured, now to be endured no more forever; of his once naked and starving children, now clad and fed comfortably; of a wife long weighed down with woe, weeping, and a broken heart, now restored to health, happiness, and a renewed affection; and how easily it is all done, once it is resolved to be done; how simple his language!—there is a logic and an eloquence in it that few with human feelings can resist. They cannot say that he desires a union of church and state, for he is not a church member; they cannot say he is vain of hearing himself speak, for his whole demeanor shows he would gladly avoid

134

speaking at all; they cannot say he speaks for pay, for he receives none, and asks for none. Nor can his sincerity in any way be doubted, or his sympathy for those he would persuade to imitate his example be denied.—*Temperance Address*, February 22, 1842.

2. When the dram-seller and drinker were incessantly told—not in accents of entreaty and persuasion, diffidently addressed by erring man to an erring brother, but in the thundering tones of anathema and denunciation with which the lordly judge often groups together all the crimes of the felon's life, and thrusts them in his face just ere he passes sentence of death upon him—that they were the authors of all the vice and misery and crime in the land; that they were the manufacturers and material of all the thieves and robbers and murderers that infest the earth; that their houses were the workshops of the devil; and that their persons should be shunned by all the good and virtuous, as moral pestilences—I say, when they were told all this, and in this way, it is not wonderful that they were slow, very slow, to acknowledge the truth of such denunciations, and to join the ranks of their denouncers in a hue and cry against themselves.

To have expected them to do otherwise than they did—to have expected them not to meet denunciation with denunciation, crimination with crimination, and anathema with anathema—was to expect a reversal of human nature, which is God's decree and can never be reversed.—*Temperance Address*, February 22, 1842.

3. But if it be true, as I have insisted, that those

135

who have suffered by intemperance personally, and have reformed, are the most powerful and efficient instruments to push the reformation to ultimate success, it does not follow that those who have not suffered have no part left them to perform. Whether or not the world would be vastly benefited by a total and final banishment from it of all intoxicating drinks seems to me not now an open question. Three fourths of mankind confess the affirmative with their tongues, and, I believe, all the rest acknowledge it in their hearts.

Ought any, then, to refuse their aid in doing what good the good of the whole demands? Shall he who cannot do much be for that reason excused if he do nothing? "But," says one, "what good can I do by signing the pledge? I never drink, even without signing." This question has already been asked and answered more than a million times. Let it be answered once more. For the man suddenly or in any other way to break off from the use of drams, who has indulged in them for a long course of years, and until his appetite for them has grown ten- or hundred-fold stronger, and more craving than any natural appetite can be, requires a most powerful moral effort. In such an undertaking he needs every moral support and influence that can possibly be brought to his aid and thrown around him. And not only so, but every moral prop should be taken from whatever argument might rise in his mind to lure him to his backsliding. When he casts his eyes around him, he should be able to see all that he respects, all that he admires, all that he loves, kindly and anxiously pointing him onward, and none beckoning him back to his former miserable "wallowing in the mire."—*Temperance Address*, February 22, 1842.

4. Gentlemen, let us drink to our mutual good health in this wholesome drink which God has given us. It is the only drink I permit in my family and in all conscience let me not depart from this custom on this occasion. It is the purest Adam's ale, from the spring.—*Reply to the Committee from Chicago Convention*, May 19, 1860.

5. I think that the reasonable men of the world have long since agreed that intemperance is one of the greatest, if not the very greatest, of all evils among mankind. That is not a matter of dispute, I believe. That the disease exists, and that it is a very great one, is agreed upon by all.—*Reply to the Sons of Temperance*, September 29, 1863.

SEE ALSO: Liquor.

TERRITORY

We have no clear and certain way of determining or demonstrating how fast territory is needed by the necessities of the country. Whoever wants to go out filibustering, then, thinks that more territory is needed. Whoever wants wider slave-fields feels sure that some additional territory is needed as slave territory. Then it is easy to show the necessity of additional slave territory as it is to assert anything that is incapable of absolute demonstration. Whatever motive a man or a set of men have for making annexation of property or territory, it is very easy to assert, but much less easy to disprove, that it is necessary for the wants of the country.—*Reply at Galesburg Debate,* October 7, 1858.

SEE ALSO: Nation 2.

THANKSGIVING

The year that is drawing toward its close has been filled with the blessings of fruitful fields and healthful skies. To these bounties, which are so constantly enjoyed that we are prone to forget the source from which they come, others have been added, which are of so extraordinary a nature that they cannot fail to penetrate and soften the heart which is habitually insensible to the ever-watchful providence of almighty God. In the midst of a civil war of unequal magnitude and severity, which has sometimes seemed to foreign states to invite and provoke their aggressions, peace has been preserved with all nations, order has been maintained, the laws have been respected and obeyed, and harmony has prevailed everywhere, except in the theater of military conflict; while that theater has been greatly contracted by the advancing armies and navies of the Union.

Needful diversions of wealth and of strength from the fields of peaceful industry to the national defense have not arrested the plow, the shuttle, or the ship; the ax has enlarged the borders of our settlements,

And the mines, as well of iron and coal as of the precious metals, have yielded even more abundantly than heretofore. Population has steadily increased, notwithstanding the waste that has been made in the camp, the siege, and the battlefield, and the country, rejoicing in the consciousness of augmented strength and vigor, is permitted to expect continuance of years with large increase of freedom.

No human counsel hath devised, nor hath any mortal hand worked out these great things. They are the gracious gifts of the most high God, who, while dealing with us in anger for our sins, hath nevertheless remembered mercy.

It has seemed to me fit and proper that they should be solemnly, reverently, and gratefully acknowledged as with one heart and one voice by the whole American people. I do, therefore, invite my fellow-citizens in every part of the United States, and also those who are at sea and those who are sojourning in foreign lands, to set apart and observe the last Thursday of November next as a day of thanksgiving and praise to our beneficent Father who dwelleth in the heavens. And I recommend to them that, while offering up the ascriptions justly due to Him for such singular deliverances and blessings, they do also, with humble penitence for our national perverseness and disobedience, commend to His tender care all those who have become widows, orphans, mourners, or sufferers in the lamentable civil strife in which we are unavoidably engaged, and fervently implore the interposition of the almighty hand to heal the wounds of the nation, and to restore it, as soon as may be consistent with the Divine purposes, to the full enjoyment of peace, harmony, tranquillity, and union.— *Thanksgiving Proclamation*, October 3, 1863.

THEORY

Practice proves more than theory, in any case.— *Annual Message to Congress*, December 1, 1862.

TRUTH

1. Truth is your truest friend, no matter what the circumstances are.—*Letter to G. E. Pickett*, February 22, 1842.

2. I planted myself upon the truth and the truth only, so far as I knew it, or could be brought to know it.—*Springfield Speech*, July 17, 1858.

3. Truth is generally the best vindication against slander.—*Letter to Secretary E. M. Stanton*, July 14, 1864.

SEE ALSO: Conduct 4; Deceit 1; Falsehood; History 3.

– U –

UNION

1. We do not want to dissolve the Union; you shall not.—*Speech at Galena,* August 1, 1856.

2. Continue to execute all the express provisions of our national Constitution, and the Union will endure forever—it being impossible to destroy it except by some action not provided for in the instrument itself.—*First Inaugural Address,* March 4, 1861.

3. I would save the Union. I would save it the shortest way under the Constitution. The sooner the national authority can be restored, the nearer the Union will be "the Union as it was." If there be those who would not save the Union unless they could at the same time save slavery, I do not agree with them. If there be those who would not save the Union unless they could at the same time destroy slavery, I do not agree with them. My paramount object in this struggle is to save the Union, and is not either to save or to destroy slavery. If I could save the Union without freeing any slave, I would do

it; and if I could save it by freeing all the slaves, I would do it; and if I could save it by freeing some and leaving others alone, I would also do that. What I do about slavery and the colored race, I do because I believe it helps to save the Union; and what I forbear, I forbear because I do not believe it would help to save the Union. I shall do less whenever I shall believe what I am doing hurts the cause, and I shall do more whenever I shall believe doing more will help the cause. I shall try to correct errors when shown to be errors, and I shall adopt new views so fast as they shall appear to be true views. I have here stated my purpose according to my view of official duty; and I intend no modification of my oft-expressed personal wish that all men everywhere could be free.—*Letter to H. Greeley,* August 22, 1862.

4. No service can be more praiseworthy and honorable than that which is rendered for the maintenance of the Constitution and Union, and the consequent preservation of free government.—*Proclamation concerning Aliens,* May 8, 1863.

SEE ALSO: Civil War 1; Government 5; Patriotism 3; Peace 3, 4; Right and Wrong 4; States 2.

– V –

VOTING

1. In all our rejoicings, let us neither express nor cherish any hard feelings toward any citizen who, by his vote, has differed with us. Let us at all times remember that all American citizens are brothers of a common country, and should dwell together in bonds of fraternal feeling.—*Remarks at the Meeting in Springfield,* November 20, 1860.

2. It is not the qualified voters, but the qualified voters who choose to vote, that constitute the political power of the State.—*An Opinion on the Admission of West Virginia into the Union,* December 31, 1862.

SEE ALSO: Ballots; Citizens; Self-government 3; Slander; Slavery 19.

– W –

WAR

1. I sincerely wish war was an easier and pleasanter business than it is; but it does not admit of holidays. —*Letter to T. H. Clay,* October 8, 1862.

2. The law of nations, and the usages and customs of war, as carried on by civilized powers, permit no distinction as to color in the treatment of prisoners of war as public enemies. To sell or enslave any captured person on account of his color, and for no offence against the laws of war, is a relapse into barbarism, and a crime against the civilization of the age.—*Order of Retaliation,* July 30, 1863.

3. Actual war coming, blood grows hot, and blood is spilled. Thought is forced from old channels into confusion. Deception breeds and thrives. Confidence dies and universal suspicion reigns. Each man feels an impulse to kill his neighbor, lest he be first killed by him. Revenge and retaliation follow. And all this, as before said, may be among honest men only; but this is not all. Every foul bird comes abroad and every dirty reptile rises up. These add crime to confusion. Strong measures deemed indispensable, but harsh at best, such men make worse by maladministration. Murders for old grudges, and murders for pelf, proceed under any cloak that will best cover for the occa-

sion.—*Letter to C. D. Drake and Others,* October 5, 1863.

4. War, at its best, is terrible, and this war of ours, in its magnitude and in its duration, is one of the most terrible. It has deranged business, totally in many localities and partially in all localities. It has destroyed property and ruined homes; it has produced a national debt and taxation unprecedented, at least in this country; it has carried mourning to almost every home, until it can almost be said that the "heavens are hung in black." Yet the war continues. . . .

It is a pertinent question, often asked in the mind privately, and from one to the other, when is the war to end? Surely I feel as deep an interest in this question as any other can; but I do not wish to name a day, a month, or year, when it is to end. I do not wish to run any risk of seeing the time come without our being ready for the end, for fear of disappointment because the time had come and not the end. We accepted this war for an object, a worthy object, and the war will end when that object is attained. Under God, I hope it never will end until that time.—*Speech at Sanitary Fair,* June 16, 1864.

5. Fondly do we hope—fervently do we pray—that this mighty scourge of war may speedily pass away.—*Second Inaugural Address,* March 4, 1865.

SEE ALSO: Ballots 3; Soldiers.

WEALTH

1. I take it that it is best for all to leave each man free to acquire property as fast as he can. Some will

get wealthy. I don't believe in a law to prevent a man from getting rich; it would do more harm than good. So while we do not propose any war upon capital, we do wish to allow the humblest man an equal chance to get rich with everybody else. When one starts poor, as most do in the race of life, free society is such that he knows he can better his condition; he knows that there is no fixed condition of labor for his whole life. . . . I want every man to have a chance.—*Speech at New Haven,* March 6, 1860.

2. Wealth is simply a superfluity of what we don't need.—*Letter to D. R. Locke,* October 12, 1864.

SEE ALSO: Civil War 4.

WELFARE

I do not mean to say that this General Government is charged with the duty of redressing or preventing all the wrongs in the world; but I do think that it is charged with preventing and redressing all wrongs which are wrongs to itself. This government is expressly charged with the duty of providing for the general welfare.—*Speech at Cincinnati,* September 17, 1859.

WILL

Will springs from the two elements of moral sense and self-interest.—*Springfield Speech,* June 26, 1857.

SEE ALSO: People 6.

WITNESS

We better know there is fire whence we see much smoke rising than we could know it by one or two witnesses swearing to it. The witnesses may commit perjury, but the smoke cannot.—*Letter to J. R. Underwood and H. Grider,* October 26, 1864.

WOMEN

I am not accustomed to the use of language of eulogy; I have never studied the art of paying compliments to women; but I must say that if all that has been said by orators and poets since the creation of the world in praise of women were applied to the women of America, it could not do them justice for their conduct during this war. I will close by saying, God bless the women of America.—*Remarks at Sanitary Fair in Washington,* March 18, 1864.

SEE ALSO: Marriage 1, 2; Slander.

WORDS

Solomon says there is "a time to keep silence," and when men wrangle by the months with no certainty that they mean the same thing, while using the same word, it perhaps were as well if they would keep silence. The words "coercion" and "invasion" are much used in these days, and often with some temper and hot blood. Let us make sure, if we can, that we do not misunderstand the meaning of those who use them. Let us get exact definition of these words, not from dictionaries, but from the men themselves, who certainly deprecate the things they would represent by the use of words.—*Remarks to the Indiana Legislature,* February 12, 1861.

SEE ALSO: Meaning.

WORK

1. Half-finished work generally proves to be labor lost.—*Address to the People of Sangamon County,* March 9, 1832.

2. If you intend to go to work, there is no better place than right where you are; if you do not intend to go to work, you cannot get along anywhere.— *Letter to J. D. Johnston,* November 4, 1851.

3. Work, work, work, is the main thing.—*Letter to J. M. Brockman,* September 25, 1860.

4. Wanting to work is so rare a want that it should be encouraged.—*A Note to Major Ramsay,* October 17, 1861.

5. I am always for the man who wishes to work.— *Endorsement of Application for Employment,* August 15, 1864.

SEE ALSO: Invention 2; Labor 4; Skill.

WORKINGMEN

1. The workingmen are the basis of all governments, for the plain reason that they are the most numerous.—*Address to Germans at Cincinnati,* February 12, 1861.

2. The strongest bond of human sympathy, outside of the family relation, should be one uniting all working people, of all nations, and tongues, and kindreds.—*Reply to Workingmen of New York,* March 21, 1864.

WRITING

Writing, the art of communicating thoughts to the mind through the eye, is the great invention of the world. Great is the astonishing range of analysis and combination which necessarily underlies the most crude and general conception of it—great, very great, in enabling us to converse with the dead, the absent, and the unborn, at all distances of time and space . . . When we remember that words are sounds merely, we shall conclude that the idea of representing those sounds by marks, so that whoever should at any time after see the marks would understand what sounds they meant, was a bold and ingenious conception, not likely to occur to one man in a million in the run of a thousand years. And when it did occur, a distinct mark for each word, giving twenty thousand different marks first to be learned, and afterward to be remembered, would follow as the second thought, and would present such a difficulty as would lead to the conclusion that the whole thing was impracticable. But the necessity still would exist; and we may readily suppose that the idea was conceived, and lost, and reproduced, and dropped, and taken up again and again, until at last the thought of dividing sounds into parts, and making a mark, not to represent a whole sound, but only a part of one, and then of combining those marks, not very many in number, upon principles of permutation, so as to represent any and all of the whole twenty thousand words, and even any additional number, was somehow conceived and pushed into practice. This was the invention of phonetic writing, as distinguished from the clumsy picture-writing of some of the nations.—*Lecture before the Springfield Library Association,* February 22, 1860.

– Y –

YOUNG AMERICA*

We have all heard of Young America. He is the most current youth of the age. Some think him conceited and arrogant; but has he not reason to entertain a rather extensive opinion of himself? Is he not the inventor and owner of the present, and sole hope of the future? Men and things, everywhere, are ministering unto him. . . . He owns a large part of the world, by right of possessing it, and all the rest by right of wanting it, and intending to have it. As Plato had for the immortality of the soul, so Young America has "a pleasing hope, a fond desire—a longing after" territory. He has a great passion—a perfect rage—for the "new"; particularly new men for office. . . . He is a great friend of humanity; and his desire for land is not selfish, but merely an impulse to extend the area of freedom. He is very anxious to fight for the liberation of enslaved nations and colonies,

---

* This is the name assumed at that time by supporters of Senator Stephen A. Douglas.

150

provided, always, they have land, and have not any liking for his interference. As to those who have no land, and would be glad of help from any quarter, he considers they can afford to wait a few hundred years longer. In knowledge he is particularly rich. He knows all that can possibly be known; inclines to believe in spiritual wrappings, and is the unquestioned inventor of "Manifest Destiny." His horror is for all that is old, particularly "Old Fogy;" and if there be anything old which he can endure, it is only old whisky and old tobacco.

If the said Young America really is, as he claims to be, the owner of all present, it must be admitted that he has considerable advantage of Old Fogy. Take, for instance, the first of all fogies, Father Adam. There he stood, a very physical man, as poets and painters inform us; but he must have been very ignorant and simple in his habits. He had had no sufficient time to learn much by observation, and he had no near neighbors to teach him anything. No part of his breakfast had been brought from the other side of the world; and it is quite probable he had no conception of the world having any other side. In all these things, it is very plain, he was no equal of Young America; the most that can be said is that according to his chance he may have been quite as much of a man as his very self-complacent descendant. Little as was what he knew, let the youngster discard all he has learned from others, and then show, if he can, any advantage on his side. . . . The great difference between Young

151

America and Old Fogy is the result of discoveries, inventions, and improvements. These, in turn, are the result of observation, reflection, and experiment.— *Lecture on "Discoveries, Inventions, and Improvements," c. February 22, 1859.*

YOUNG MEN

The way for a young man to rise is to improve himself every way he can, never suspecting that anybody wishes to hinder him.—*Letter to W. H. Herndon,* July 10, 1848.

SEE ALSO: Lawyers; Self-government 3.